"In his first major Christian book, Mark Lanier brings to Christian publishing the same expertise, communication skills and pure, enthusiastic joy for the subject that he has brought to courtrooms and TV-network interviews across America for decades. But most folks don't know that Mark is as good a theologian and Christian communicator as he is a trial attorney. In some ways this book is a modern *Evidence That Demands a Verdict*. It is an excellent read for anyone who wants to see the evidence for the basic objective truths of Christian faith."

John Michael Talbot, author of *The Jesus Prayer*

"Historians, scientists and lawyers are after the same thing: to discover what really happened. Mark Lanier, one of America's best lawyers, introduces us to history's expert witnesses regarding our most profound questions and tells a compelling story sure to convince any jury."

David B. Capes, Thomas Nelson Research Professor, Houston Baptist University

"Because Mark Lanier is my Sunday school teacher, I have the joy of following his teaching week by week no matter where I am in the world. I eventually print out every lesson for my own reference because he is the quintessential teacher, using every means to invest his discerning exposition and wonderful insights into those of us who follow his teaching. I look forward to this volume not only for my personal edification but also as a book that I can place in the hands of those seeking to know Christ in a personal way and to grow in the Christian faith."

Dorothy Kelley Patterson, professor of theology in women's studies, Southwestern Baptist Theological Seminary, Fort Worth, Texas

"Mark Lanier, a noted lawyer and Bible scholar, deftly takes the reader through a carefully argued case for Christianity. Presenting testimony of key witnesses for and cross-examining opponents of the Christian faith, he makes a compelling case. The fair-minded reader will be persuaded that the preponderance of evidence supports the claims of the New Testament about the life, death and resurrection of Jesus of Nazareth."

James K. Hoffmeier, professor of Old Testament and Near Eastern archaeology, Trinity International University

"Mark Lanier is uniquely qualified to give God a fair hearing today. His skills as a trial lawyer are renowned. So too is his apologetical persuasiveness and winsome delivery. When you combine these gifts you hear a lawyer's examination of the claims of Christianity and an evangelist's appeal for a decision. *Christianity on Trial* is a great read for any wishing to examine the compelling evidence about Jesus Christ and reach a verdict about his claim on people's lives."

Simon Vibert, vice principal, Wycliffe Hall, Oxford

"Trial lawyers are often noted for incisive analysis, broad knowledge and the ability to spot the weakness in the opposition's argument. Mark Lanier demonstrates every one of these instincts in *Christianity on Trial*. His expertise in using the biblical languages uniquely qualifies him to ask—and answer—all the really tough questions. As a fresh assessment of the intellectual validity of the Christian, this book will delight pastors, theologians, church members and even critics."

Paige Patterson, Southwestern Baptist Theological Seminary, Fort Worth, Texas

"Mark Lanier has probably read more about the Bible than many biblical scholars and combines this with his experience as a leading trial lawyer. The result is a gripping read and a compelling case for Christianity. He touches on so many different kinds of argument that there is something for everyone in this feast."

Peter Williams, warden, Tyndale House, Cambridge, United Kingdom

"Authored by one of the nation's leading trial lawyers, *Christianity on Trial* brilliantly employs the truth-finding methods of the legal process to produce an eminently readable, highly persuasive work of Christian apologetics. This is an extraordinary trial lawyer's version of *Mere Christianity*. In his inimitable fashion, Mark Lanier combines his superb expertise as a courtroom lawyer with profound knowledge of biblical scholarship and thoughtful reflection on daily life. Fearless in tackling the most difficult matters of belief, this engaging book speaks to all those interested in seeking truth—whether in the courtroom, in the library or in everyday life."

Ken Starr, president, Baylor University

Tom & Brenda —
May God bless you both deeply
Mark

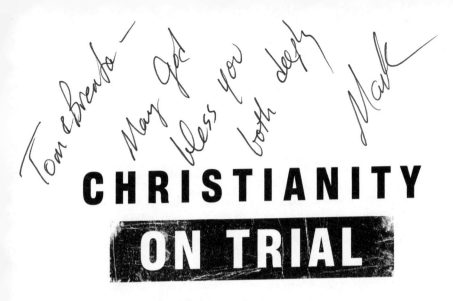

CHRISTIANITY
ON TRIAL

A LAWYER EXAMINES *the* CHRISTIAN FAITH

W. MARK LANIER

IVP Books

An imprint of InterVarsity Press
Downers Grove, Illinois

InterVarsity Press
P.O. Box 1400, Downers Grove, IL 60515-1426
www.ivpress.com
email@ivpress.com

InterVarsity Press® is the book-publishing division of InterVarsity Christian Fellowship/USA®, a movement of students and faculty active on campus at hundreds of universities, colleges and schools of nursing in the United States of America, and a member movement of the International Fellowship of Evangelical Students. For information about local and regional activities, write Public Relations Dept., InterVarsity Christian Fellowship/USA, 6400 Schroeder Rd., P.O. Box 7895, Madison, WI 53707-7895, or visit the IVCF website at www.intervarsity.org.

Scripture quotations, unless otherwise noted, are from The Holy Bible, English Standard Version, copyright © 2001 by Crossway Bibles, a division of Good News Publishers. Used by permission. All rights reserved.

While all stories in this book are true, some names and identifying information in this book have been changed to protect the privacy of the individuals involved.

Cover design: David Fassett

Interior design: Beth Hagenberg

Images: Andrew Unangst/Getty Images

    ©procurator/iStockphoto

    photo of Adolf Hitler visiting the Nietzsche Archive in Weimar, October 1935: bpk, Berlin / Art Resource, NY. Used by permission.

ISBN 978-0-8308-3667-3 (print)
ISBN 978-0-8308-9634-9 (digital)

Printed in the United States of America ∞

Library of Congress Cataloging-in-Publication Data

Lanier, W. Mark, 1960-
  Christianity on trial : a lawyer examines the Christian faith / W. Mark Lanier.
     pages cm
  Includes bibliographical references.
  ISBN 978-0-8308-3667-3 (pbk. : alk. paper)
  1. Apologetics. I. Title.
  BT1103.L36 2014
  239—dc23

                                            2014009323

| P | 19 | 18 | 17 | 16 | 15 | 14 | 13 | 12 | 11 | 10 | 9 | 8 | 7 | 6 | 5 | 4 | 3 | 2 | 1 |
| Y | 30 | 29 | 28 | 27 | 26 | 25 | 24 | 23 | 22 | 21 | 20 | 19 | 18 | 17 | 16 | 15 | 14 |

Contents

Dedication and Acknowledgments

I DEDICATE THIS WORK TO my marvelous wife, Becky, and our five special children, Will, Gracie, Rachel, Rebecca and Sarah. They are God's gracious gifts in my life that continually show me the joys of family and love.

I also acknowledge and thank my godly mother and my father, who awaits us in God's kingdom, for an upbringing that taught of God and always encouraged questioning and thinking about truth and reality.

My thanks go to the many supporters and friends, including the pastoral staff at our church (David Fleming and Stephen Trammel), where I first taught much of this material. Many people commented on those lessons as I wrote and delivered them each week in our Life Groups. For those voices, thank you for making this book better.

I also thank the marvelous people at InterVarsity Press for publishing this work, especially Al Hsu and Drew Blankman. They, along with Charles Mickey of the Lanier Theological Library, improved this product significantly.

More information on my class, including video presentations of the material in this book and the resources I use in this and other writings, can be found at the class website, www.biblical-literacy .org, and at our library website, www.LanierTheologicalLibrary.org.

Preface

LAST WEEK STARTED OUT SUPREMELY BUSY. Sunday morning, I taught my class at church and went to a big family lunch. Immediately afterward, I left Houston for a 6 p.m. meeting in Chicago. A troop of lawyers convened to assist in my preparations for a deposition I was taking the next day. (A deposition is an examination of a witness under oath that has all the trappings of a trial except it doesn't occur in a courtroom and the judge is not present. Video cameras capture the event, and a court reporter takes down each word. That testimony can later be played by video or read into evidence at a trial.)

We holed up in a hotel conference room and went past midnight. Juan Wilson, my trusted friend and coworker, brought in dinner so we could work without losing any time. I was about to take the deposition of a design engineer who had led a team developing a metal hip implant. We believed the implant was poorly designed, and obvious safety warnings were ignored in an effort to secure a worldwide market that put over a billion dollars into the company's hands. The implants were taken off the market because of their dangers, but not before being placed in hundreds of thousands of unknowing victims. This deposition would cover issues of metal corrosion, testing protocols, the effects of metal debris in the body, ions and nanoparticles, and more.

I was up early Monday morning to do final preparation, and I began the deposition at 9:03. We worked through lunch, and the deposition ended midafternoon. We were taking the deposition at a hotel by the airport, which enabled me to quickly get out of Chicago and on to the next destination. I had to be at a reception in Scottsdale, Arizona, that night.

The reception in Scottsdale went well, but I had to leave it by 8:30 p.m. to return to the airport and get to Santa Ana, California. In Santa Ana I had a meeting late into the night in preparation for a federal court hearing scheduled to begin promptly at 8 a.m. It was what lawyers call a *Daubert* hearing. This name comes from a famous case (Daubert was the name of the plaintiff), and it determines whether an expert's testimony is going to be allowed at a trial.

In American courts the judge is deemed the gatekeeper to the jury, and a jury is not allowed to hear expert testimony unless the judge deems it reliable. The purpose is to keep junk science out of a courtroom. This was a high-profile trial concerning whether a major brand of car would at times accelerate even when the brakes were engaged. The judge would be scrutinizing each expert and each opinion very carefully, as the media watched from the gallery.

After a brief night's sleep, I was up and standing in line to make it through courthouse metal detectors by 7:15. The judge kept us until 1 p.m., with two ten-minute breaks allowed. Our team then met in the courthouse café over coffees and Diet Cokes for another hour of planning.

From there I hustled back to the airport to get back to Scottsdale, Arizona, where I was scheduled to give a dinner speech to a seminar full of lawyers. I arrived with just enough time to clean up and change clothes. I went into the dinner wiped out. It had already been a long week, and I was running on just a few hours of sleep.

At the appropriate time I gave my dinner speech. Afterward, I finished dinner and hoped to retire to my room. (I had two hours of presentations I had to make the next morning, followed immediately by an expert coming to meet with me on matters of pharmaceutical sales practices. I was hoping to get some sleep before waking up early enough to get the PowerPoint done for the speeches. I also had the expert's ninety-one-page report to read before the next day began.) I politely excused myself and got up from my table to head back to my room. As I was walking out, a lawyer I had met at the reception the night before got up from his table and came to me. He asked me how my *Daubert* hearing had gone. I told him I thought it went well, and he then informed me that he had been on my website after meeting me. I smiled, wanting to be polite and wanting to go to sleep. He then said he had been on my "Bible website," not just my law firm website. I found that a bit surprising. Looking me dead in the eye, he proclaimed, "I am an agnostic. Give me the *Daubert* hearing on God!"

He was using lawyer jargon to ask me for evidence on why believing in God has any legitimacy. I smiled while his request sank in. Before I could say anything, I realized five other lawyers and one spouse were standing nearby and forming a chorus saying, "Yes, we would like to hear this too!"

It was like someone flipped a switch in me. There is something invigorating about declaring the wonders of God. That is not to say that sleep is unimportant. Nor that drowsiness cannot trump even the greatest opportunity to discuss God, but it is invigorating nonetheless.

Any sense of fatigue left me. I told those interested that I would *love* to give them a *Daubert* hearing on my faith! Each grabbed a chair, and we sat for well over an hour while I worked through probing questions about God, faith, science, the Bible, Adam and Eve, creation and evolution, and, most important, the work of Jesus and the relationship that he makes possible. The people in the group identified themselves as atheist, agnostic, two Reformed Jews, new age and uncertain. The conversation was rich, and I counted it a blessing to be a part of it. (I am continuing my dialogue with several of these people by email.)

Before the evening was over, I told them about this book, which is basically a *Daubert* hearing on core elements of the Christian faith. Is it reasonable to believe in God? If so, what kind of God is he? What are the implications of such a belief? Does it affect who we are and what we are doing? Does it explain life? Does it give life meaning?

Each of my new friends expressed a desire to read this book. My hope is that it serves as a catalyst for further discussions with them and with others who read it as well. I look forward to where God may lead these conversations.

Introduction

IS IT REASONABLE TO BELIEVE IN GOD? Can God be infinite, personal and moral? What are the implications of people being made in his image? Is it intellectually honest to believe that the Bible is God's revelation to humanity? Do people have an ability to make real choices, or are we simply products of our DNA in combination with our environment? Does a belief in a historical Jesus who died and was physically resurrected pass the test of common sense? Should we expect the eventual return of Jesus and life after death?

These questions probe the core of the Christian faith. They are real questions for real people living in a real world. They are questions that make a difference. They are the basic questions I explore in this book.

What business does a trial lawyer have examining the Christian faith? Isn't that the jurisdiction of the theologian? What can a trial lawyer bring to the discussion that is not more carefully or artfully covered by the "experts"?

These challenging questions have occupied many of humanity's best minds for centuries. Debating the existence of God or what kind of God she or he is, is not new. Nor is asking whether the Bible is God's Word. Through millennia great minds have sought to discover truth and determine what makes "right" right and "wrong" wrong. Are these really the questions we want a trial lawyer to examine? Can we learn anything by putting these issues on trial?

Perhaps not! But before you dismiss the idea, let this lawyer provide a defense. The American courtroom is an amazing development. It has one ultimate goal: discovery of truth. The question for every jury boils down to "what truly happened?" To find truth, civilization has learned a number of things are necessary. Most important, there must be a fair playing field. Jurors should be fair. Judges should be fair. Even the lawyers are charged to be fair and honest in finding and presenting evidence. Because of this, courtrooms have evolved strict rules of engagement to allow lawyers the freedom to develop evidence and then put the evidence on public display. From that display jurors are able to look at the evidence and assess it. Experience has indicated that there is no other human institution that can so readily sift through and weigh information to derive trustworthy conclusions.

Someone who reads this will say, "Objection, counselor! The scientist's lab or the mathematician's calculation is the best place to derive truth." Yes and no. Hard sciences and mathematics do tell us provable facts like two plus two is four, but we must distinguish what is provable in the lab from what is not.

Laboratories are marvelous places to answer questions of chemistry, physics and biology. But can you answer "Who ran the red light?" with test tubes and a calculator? No. Not even when we are confident that someone indeed did run a red light. That answer is best found from an investigation of evidence, eyewitness accounts, pictures, examining the scene, evaluating the skid marks and so forth. That investigation then goes to a jury or judge who is first found to be fair and unbiased. The judge and jury, upon presentation of the evidence, then draw a conclusion based on common sense, logic and life experiences.

Do judges and juries always get it right? Of course not. The legal system can break down. Yet most jurists will confirm what studies have repeatedly found to be true. The American judicial system, when operating properly under its rules, is the best system society has devised for answering such questions. When the courts fail, generally it is not the fault of the system but rather of a jury or judge. The system works remarkably well, as long as judges and juries remain unbiased. They must be fair in weighing the evidence.

So is science the laboratory for testing faith? No. The issues of history are core to faith, and they rarely are answerable in a laboratory.

Trial lawyers live in a world of issues and questions that are bigger than any laboratory could ever address. In the world of trial lawyers, laboratory truths help. They are frequently key ingredients to more complicated recipes. Hard facts of science are part of a jury's basis for ultimate decisions. DNA evidence is a tool in determining whether someone is fairly implicated in a crime. The laws of physics help reveal whether someone was speeding at the time of a crash.

The real hard decisions, those that tap the sciences, are "Who did it?" and "What happened?" decisions. These are decisions that make a difference in life or death. These decisions can put people in prison or bankruptcy. These decisions utilize the tools of science, but juries, not a laboratory, make the hard conclusions. Common, ordinary people sit down, analyze the evidence, discuss their opinions and decide the truth.

In this process the lawyer plays an integral role. The lawyer first gathers and sorts through the evidence. The importance of that process cannot be overstated. Lawyers call it the "discovery phase" of a trial. For every hour in court, I spend over forty hours re-

searching and investigating. For example, before the final preparation session for taking the engineer's deposition I discussed in the
preface, I spent roughly five hundred hours studying the subject. I
pored through documents, met for days learning from eight of the
world's top engineers, read scores of studies and worked through
the science meticulously. This is all part of the "discovery phase."

This serves two goals. First, I must understand the science well
enough to cross-examine the witnesses working for the other side.
So, for example, in a benzene exposure case I recently tried, it was
not enough that I was able to explain how the benzene led to a
young man's leukemia. I also had to cross-examine a set of opposing
experts who were arguing the benzene was unrelated.

Second, as a lawyer I must be able to present complicated expert
testimony in such a way that it makes sense to nonexperts. But this
cannot be done at the expense of accuracy. Things cannot be over-
simplified such that it becomes anything less than dead-on right.
That is all an appellate court would need to throw out the jury's
decision and invalidate five years or more of hard work.

This "discovery" stage is broad. Lawyers are allowed to discover
not only relevant evidence but also evidence that might lead to
relevant evidence. It cannot become a fishing expedition, but unlike
in a trial, every question does not have to be directly relevant itself.

A trial is different. In a trial, only relevant evidence comes before
a jury. It is the judge's responsibility to decide what evidence is
relevant and what is not. As I present evidence in a trial, the court
often requires me to explain the relevance along the way. Failure to
do so leaves me open to "Objection: relevance," with the judge
responding, "Sustained."

A good example is the hip case I mentioned in the preface. I am
conducting discovery to document what was known about the
effect that metal ions and nanoparticle debris have on the human

body. Sometimes people who have artificial hips made of a metal ball in a metal liner/socket experience elevated levels of these metals that kill surrounding tissues. I need to know what the implant company knew or, through the exercise of reasonable diligence, should have known about the potential for this damage. While delving into two decades of emails, presentations, correspondence, files and experiments, I have found lots of fascinating and even damaging evidence that is not really relevant to my issue. Will that evidence get to a jury? No.

This is why I have presented the case as I have in this book. Some of the chapters are arguments. Others are more educational. The educational chapters are setting out important matters and a framework that becomes relevant in later chapters. It is my effort to stop a "relevance" objection before it is lodged!

Some might think trial work is simply lawyer hocus-pocus. As if through some sleight of hand (or better yet, through slick words), lawyers seduce the unwary public into supporting a position. Nothing could be further from the truth. Courts have rules that are rigorously enforced, rules that apply to the evidence under consideration as well as the arguments made by lawyers. Judges follow rules shaped over the last six hundred years in determining what evidence is authentic, authoritative, relevant and proper for consideration.

Are there ever absurd results? Occasionally, but not as often as one might think! The public only hears of the bizarre cases, not the millions of cases where the system works. Furthermore, those rare glitches are always subject to appellate review. This allows a set of judges to reassess the evidence and rules to see if justice went awry.

Over time, lawyers develop good habits about how to do their job. There are rules we tend to live by. We know better than to trust unreliable sources. We know that tabloid headlines are rarely true. We know that nothing substitutes for getting past hearsay to the original evidence. Consistency is prized; inconsistency is abhorred. The principle of Occam's Razor applies to the courtroom too: The simpler explanation is typically more reliable than one that is unnecessarily complicated (at least if the simple one takes into account all the evidence). We know to look carefully for agendas that might taint a witness's opinions and to weigh each witness's credibility.

I have spent thirty years as a lawyer, although I began my formal training receiving a B.A. in biblical languages. My Bible studies continued through the decades as my courtroom experience took me coast to coast trying everyday cases as well as those on the front pages of the New York Times. People frequently come to me after Googling me with one of two lines. If I am approached when I have been speaking as a lawyer, they say, "I Googled you. I had no idea you are a Christian thinker and teacher." Where I speak on matters of faith or the Bible, I often hear someone say, "I Googled you. I had no idea you are a recognized lawyer." This book is a project that intersects these two lifelong interests—faith and law.

So, give this lawyer his day in court. Let's use the basic approach of court, along with the practical judgments from decades of work. Let's put these tools to work on questioning core Christian beliefs. Then you can be the jury and cast your vote. You can decide what is reasonable and what is not.

Each trial begins with a lawyer's opening statement. From there the lawyer presents the case, calling witnesses and putting documents into evidence. Once the evidence is in, the lawyer has a chance to give a summation or closing argument. At that point, deliberations begin and a jury makes its decision.

This is the journey we will take in this book. This book will proceed with the format of a trial, but with a few practical changes. Like a trial, I will begin with an opening statement that serves as the book's introduction. There, I lay out the road map of issues and witnesses. I explain where the evidence in trial will go. After that I present the evidence. I cover the "witnesses" in a narrative fashion rather than the typical question-and-answer format of a trial. Evidence goes beyond witnesses. We will consider science, documents and the world as well—just like a trial. I will then give a summation or closing argument, where I draw conclusions from all the separate pieces of evidence.

We are missing one major component of a trial: opposing counsel. That does not mean we do not face the cynics' challenges. The public is bombarded by those skeptical about Christian faith. Those opposing my view are not silent. We can readily find television shows that question or make light of the reasonableness of Christian faith. The Internet is replete with articles, Web legends and blogs opposing most every aspect of Christianity.

So I begin this book at the trial stage. The preparation behind this book has followed the rules I would follow in legal discovery. All that remains is for me to present my opening statement, the evidence in support of my case and the closing argument to you, the reader and jury.

So I begin, "Ladies and gentlemen of the jury . . ."

1

Opening Statement

MORE TIMES THAN I CAN COUNT, I have heard the black-robed judge declare, "Mr. Lanier, you may begin your opening statement." Each time, I begin much the same. I thank the jury for their time and attention. I explain that I am going to give a brief summary of what the case is about, who the witnesses are and what is coming. The jury learns best if they know the rhyme and reason of a lawyer's presentation. So my opening begins with just that, an explanation of what I hope to accomplish and how I plan to get there.

OPENING STATEMENT

Any exploration of Christian beliefs rightfully starts with exploring whether there is a God and, if there is, what kind of God. The Christian faith rests on core beliefs about God, humanity, truth, reality, right and wrong, the responsibility of human choice, the incarnate Christ, his death, burial, and resurrection, and a coming age where things are made right and Christ's reign is apparent to all. These are issues that can and should be examined.

These issues need to be understood in light of not only the teachings of the Bible but also of the world around us. If Scripture is true, then we should be able to see its truth in the world around us. The biblical worldview should be one that makes sense of everyday life. This is a commonsense test that applies to much of everyday life. We might call it the "smell test." Does something smell right? Does it make sense with what we experience day in and day out?

Lawyers have two kinds of evidence they can present in court—direct evidence and circumstantial evidence. *Direct evidence* is something one has firsthand knowledge of. For example, if I am outside in the rain, I can affirm directly that it is raining. *Circumstantial evidence* is different. If I am in a building at the front door, and I notice that everyone who enters has a wet umbrella, wet clothes and wet shoes, then I can assess that as evidence that it is raining, even though I have not witnessed the rain directly. All I have seen are circumstances that indicate rain.

Circumstantial evidence can also affirm or contradict direct testimony. If someone tells me it is raining, and I watch people coming in with wet umbrellas, wet clothes and wet hair, the circumstances affirm what I am being told. However, if someone tells me it is raining, and people come in dry as a bone, with no rain gear, I might have my suspicions because the circumstances belie the claim of rain.

As we look at issues, especially as we weigh the skeptic's concerns, we repeatedly ask whether the facts of life are consistent with or contradict one view or another. This approach is used in chapter two, where we discuss whether it is reasonable to believe there is a God. We explore this ultimate question with a close examination of the testimony of life. We cannot examine God directly; he is not subject to a physical examination. We rely on circumstantial evidence.

We do not stop there, however. Many people recognize that some sort of divine being is possible, if not likely, but that hardly means that the God of the Bible is real. Whatever being there is—God, god or even gods—how are we to know much about him, her or them?

Is God something akin to the Force in Star Wars? Is there a divine being sitting atop a mountain that we are all climbing toward? Is God an old man, sitting in a rocker, looking down on earth and occasionally wagging a finger over some particularly tawdry sin? Is the divine a supercomputer making calculations and keeping tabs on the universe? Is God male or female? Is God such an unknown that you envision nothing? Maybe instead of envisioning God, you envision his or her traits. Is God kind? Loving? Does God have a short fuse? Is God moody or easily angered? What is your role and relationship with God? Do you ignore the divine? Do you fear God? Do you have a relationship with God? Is your relationship strained? Is God your harbor in the storms of life? Is God the kind and loving parent who is always there for you?

We need to vocalize and consider these ideas of God, and we do so by first dismissing views that, however prominent they may be, are not those of the biblical God. It is the biblical God under examination here. We are weighing the God of the Bible against the reality of life, and so we need to first explore and understand *him*. This takes on added importance because a lot of people do not believe in God, in part because of a misperception of who the Christian God is. Those perceptions merit attention.

We do not start this examination with a blank slate. We will consider the views of God we get from the witnesses that have already discussed this issue, either directly or indirectly. I will examine the writings of a now-deceased Anglican minister named J. B. Phillips, who believed that many of us carry ideas of God that are not scriptural and carefully dissected these nonbiblical views. Through his ideas we will probe the distinctions between God as many understand him and God as explained in the Bible. I will also consider the gods of Hollywood and print. We will look at *Life of Pi* and *Star Wars* to consider their images of the divine.

Following that, in chapters four and five, I set out the direct biblical testimony about who God is. Chapter three erases the whiteboard with its misperceptions about God, and chapters four and five write anew upon the board, setting out the biblical teachings of God.

Simply looking at the Bible cannot do this, because the book is rooted in everyday life and the world. So this examination will necessarily entail looking at nature. In addition to the Bible, the witnesses include the heavens as understood by modern astronomical science, Albert Einstein and British physicist Sir John Polkinghorne. These witnesses speak to the biblical God in ways that affect our understandings of the biblical God in chapter four.

In chapter five I will call a last set of witnesses to testify about God's nature. In addition to the Bible's teaching from the apostle John, I will present as evidence subatomic particles as well as the testimony of the ancient Greek philosopher Heraclitus.

After our efforts at determining the existence and nature of God, I turn the discussion to the idea that God communicates through Scripture (chap. 6). Does the idea of a divinely inspired Bible make sense? Is the Bible something that God gave to humans or something that humans made up about God? My witnesses will include the humanist Thomas Huxley, world-renowned linguist Noam Chomsky and the teachings of communication theorists. These scholars are notable for their writings on the human mind and how the brain integrates speech, communication and thought.

The next progression of examination will focus on reality and truth (chap. 7). Is our world like the one depicted in the Hollywood film *The Matrix*? Are we in a reality show like *The Truman Show*? Is what we are experiencing really real? My witnesses on this issue will include the ancient Greek philosopher Plato and the seventeenth-century French philosopher René Descartes. I will also call to the witness stand Oxford's cutting-edge philosopher Nick Bostrom, who has made a number of bold claims about possible realities we might live in. Bostrom has popularized the idea that we might actually be part of a self-conscious computer program.

I will move our examination into questions of right and wrong in chapter eight. There I will put on the stand Charles Darwin and Friedrich Nietzsche. I will also address the testimony and ideas raised by Plato's predecessor, Socrates. This evidence addresses the deplorable actions of Hitler and the Third Reich, asking, How could they have thought they were doing something right or noble? Do we dismiss the Nazis as deranged people? I suggest we should examine them and their motives, and then see what conclusions are fairly drawn from the evidence. We will examine the ideas behind the Nazi morality, comparing them to biblical truth. The big issue will then be how ideas of right and wrong are formed today—through biblical principles or those of the Third Reich?

In chapter nine I will close in on the questions of determinism and choice. Do we do things because we choose to, or is the die already cast? Are we creatures with a will that can decide on a course of action after weighing different choices, or is that decision already made simply by the chemistry of our brains combined with the external circumstances? In other words, are we chemical reactions alone, or can we truly make choices? My witnesses on this issue include the twentieth-century behavioral psychologist B. F. Skinner, whom I will cross-examine on the subject. Skinner wrote that humans are a mere mixture of chemicals reacting to a preset environment. As such, people have no freedom or dignity. Such a view removes true moral responsibility from people. How can people be held morally responsible if they can't make meaningful choices?

If choices and moral responsibility exist, then everyone stands accountable before a moral God. This sets up a problem of huge proportion. The Bible teaches that there is an answer to such a problem, and it is found in the incarnation, death and resurrection of Jesus. But Jesus' death and physical resurrection is a challenging idea for many. At first blush, it can seem quite preposterous; certainly no one alive has ever witnessed it. So in chapter ten I will examine this idea under the most careful judicial scrutiny to see if there is any reasonable basis for believing it. My witnesses will include Matthew, Mark, Luke and John, as well as others. Using rules of court, I will set out the evidence for you to decide what is credible and what is not.

Before closing in a final chapter, I will examine the idea of heaven and eternity in chapter eleven. Is it simply a pretend hope of people doomed to eventual death? Is it a pipe dream that might help us muddle through the years of life? Or is it real? Is it a reasonable conclusion to the world and reality as we know it?

In each of these areas, we will weigh the biblical claims alongside the witnesses I bring into the discussion. The goal behind our activity is to see, after due scrutiny, whether it is reasonable to believe in

- God, who is infinite, personal and moral, who has made human beings in his image, and who has communicated to humanity through revelation

- Humans as creatures who can really make choices in life

- Jesus as a human who died and was then physically resurrected and will come again in an eternal reigning kingdom

So I ask, does Christianity provide a plausible account of the universe both broadly and in its particulars? Does it explain why we are the way we are, and why things are the way they are? Does it make sense of our life experiences?

I will conclude our trial with a summation, known in legal terms as a closing argument. In that chapter we will work through the conclusions reachable from the evidence presented. We will consider the teachings of Scripture along with the world around us. We will see if science, current knowledge and common sense can combine to produce a rich understanding of God and the strength of the foundations for faith. The verdict can then be determined. Each person has to decide how to live in light of the verdict he or she reaches.

2

God? gods? Or Nothing?

I HAVE TWO GOALS TODAY. One is to write this chapter. Another is to write an opening statement for a case I begin trying in a few weeks.

This chapter concerns whether or not there is a God. The case is about whether Ms. John's car experienced "unintended acceleration." In other words, did her car accelerate, even though she was not pushing the accelerator? Ms. John says she was at a stop sign about to turn right. As she lifted her foot off the brake, before she put her foot onto the gas pedal, her car "took off like an airplane." It shot forward, and she was unable to turn right. Instead she hopped the curb before her, shot through a schoolyard, dodging the playground, and six seconds after her ordeal started, smashed into the gymnasium wall.

Ms. John says once the car took off, she immediately pressed the brake, to no avail.

The car company has taken the position that the car did no such thing. It believes that Ms. John thought she was pressing the brake, but was in fact pressing the gas pedal.

I do not have a video of Ms. John's foot. Beyond her testimony of what she thought she was doing, there is no direct testimony. There were no witnesses in the car. All I have is "circumstantial evidence" (see chap. 1). Here is what I mean.

Ms. John's health at the time was good. The EMS personnel checked her over, as did the hospital. She had diabetes, but her blood sugar tested fine. Her mental clarity was fine. There were skid marks at a place where you would expect them had she been applying the brakes. The first responders on the scene all heard her repeatedly say, "It wouldn't stop. It wouldn't stop." This car manufacturer had installed an electronic control system just a few model years earlier that accelerates the car by a computer rather than an old-fashioned cable that goes from the gas pedal to the carburetor. Since the change to the computer system, the number of complaints like Ms. John's has skyrocketed to 37,900. Ms. John was not distracted at the time—no cell phone, no eating while driving, no radio.

Now the jury will have to decide, based on the circumstances, is it more likely than not that Ms. John hit the wrong pedal, or did her car go wild?

This opening statement, which I will work on today, is not unlike this chapter. I have no immediate eyewitness to God in a physical or mystical form in front of me. I cannot subject him or some apparition to lab tests, nor can I physically tote him around to show people for their belief.

In the preface I spoke of a postdinner discussion I had with a small group of lawyers who wanted me to prove God exists. One of the lawyers was a professed agnostic, and at one point he reached out his hands to me and said, "Come join me. Leave the certainty of your faith and embrace the unknown! Be an agnostic with me. You can do it!"

I responded truly, "I am sorry. I do not have enough faith to do that! It would take too much faith to turn away from the certain belief I have about God."

He was stunned. He thought it was a leap of faith to believe in

God. It had not occurred to him that his agnosticism was a leap of faith. That I thought faith more intellectually reasonable was a foreign concept to him and several others in the group. Yet for me, it wasn't. I was quite sincere. He wanted my proof.

The proof of God must come from circumstantial evidence. We look around us and within us and ask, Is it more likely than not that there is a God? I suggest it is not only possible there is a God but also that God is the most logical answer to the world as we see and experience it. God is the best explanation for the circumstances of life, whether we are looking outward at others or inward to ourselves.

Witness List

Note: *In a trial witnesses are "called to the stand." This is because historically witnesses stood to testify. Now they sit, but the language hasn't changed. We still "call them to the stand" where their testimony is elicited in question-and-answer form. With special court permission witnesses are allowed to testify in a narrative form. Lawyers are allowed to read documents into evidence along with certain witness statements. Courts can also permit lawyers to present evidence in a summary form. In this book the "witnesses" are used as referenced, but within a narrative, not in question-and-answer format.*

King John of England (1166–1216). *John reigned as King of England from 1199 until his death. His most famous achievement was signing the Magna Carta.*

Gilbert Keith (G. K.) Chesterton (1874–1936). *Chesterton was an English writer on many subjects, including philosophy and matters of the Christian faith.*

King Ashurbanipal of Assyria (668–627 b.c.). *Ashurbanipal ruled from Nineveh, a city on the eastern bank of the Tigris River in what is now northern Iraq. During his rule, Nineveh was the largest city in the world.*

Clive Staples (C. S.) Lewis (1898–1963). *C. S. Lewis taught at both Oxford University and Cambridge University and was accomplished as an academic in English, medieval and Renaissance literature; a novelist; a broadcaster; and a lay theologian. He was an atheist into adulthood before converting first to theism and then to Christianity.*

In the history of human civilization, people have used many approaches to determine historical truth, especially in the context of making a claim open to dispute. For a while in history these questions were posed to God (or gods), with religious rituals set up to discern the answer. Throughout a great bit of history, cases of "he said–she said" were decided through duels or some other trial by battle, generally based on the idea that the gods would protect the truthful one. As civilization progressed, wise or powerful people were designated to determine the truth. Frequently, these were either associated with the secular power structure (the king or other noblemen) or the religious power structure (the clergy).

In the eleventh century Western civilization reached a milestone when William the Conqueror (c. 1028–1087) began using citizen inquests to determine and record certain financial matters. The role of ordinary citizens continued to grow in the legal system, and in 1215 a core legal document for Western society was forced on King John of England. Written in Latin and called the Magna Carta (Latin for the "Great Charter"), significant parts of this law are still on the books in England, including clause 39, which reads,

No Freeman shall be seized or imprisoned, or stripped of his rights or possessions, or outlawed, or exiled, or deprived of his standing in any other way, nor will we proceed with force against him, or send others to do so, *except by the lawful judgment of his equals* or by the law of the land. (italics added)

This was the seed from which trial by jury became a right (see fig. 2.1).

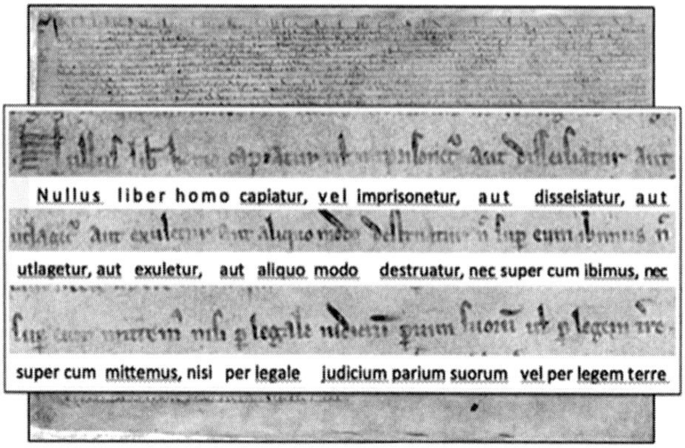

Figure 2.1. Magna Carta (photo from Wikimedia Commons; transliteration added)

Courts transitioned to having disinterested groups of ordinary citizens (initially limited to white citizen landholders) taking the role of fact finders. The value of citizens to act as the finders of fact in disputes was one of the reasons the Americans declared independence from the King of England in 1776. The Declaration of Independence justified itself with "Facts submitted to a candid world," including that of the King of England depriving the people, "in many cases, of the benefits of Trial by Jury" (see fig. 2.2).

Not surprisingly, shortly after establishing the United States of America, the Constitution was amended with a Bill of Rights that included the Seventh Amendment to ensure the right to a jury trial. "In suits at common law . . . the right of trial by jury shall be preserved, and no fact tried by jury, shall be otherwise re-examined in any Court of the United States, than according to the rules of the common law." This cornerstone of the American judicial system has its fans and critics. It is certainly not perfect, but it is still reckoned the most reliable system for determining fair and impartial findings of fact. *Finders of fact* is a phrase frequently used in legal circles for the jury. The judge, a legal scholar, is responsible for knowing and applying the law. But the determiner of facts, the ones who decide what

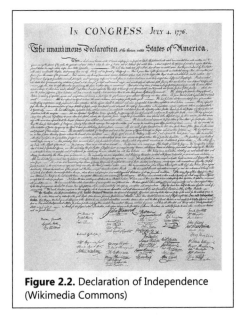

Figure 2.2. Declaration of Independence (Wikimedia Commons)

truly happened in history, is the province solely of the jury.

Generally consisting of twelve people, although sometimes only six, a jury is a group of ordinary people who bring collective memories and common experiences to bear on the decision process. In determining what ordinary events transpired (the "findings of fact"), these ordinary people trump the value of trained scholars and the world's highest intellects.

While trained scholars may disagree about whether they are more competent to uncover the facts of historical events, the historical consensus is that those experts have biases themselves, generally from a focus that is only through their academic lens. A jury, on the other hand, has the benefits of listening to experts and of hearing pros and cons, and the opportunity to comprehend, assess and determine what is more likely or not the truth.

The English writer G. K. Chesterton wrote on many subjects,

including philosophy, politics and Christianity (see fig. 2.3). Regarding the jury system, he wrote:

Figure 2.3. G. K. Chesterton (Wikimedia Commons)

Our civilization has decided, and very justly decided, that determining the guilt or innocence of a man is a thing too important to be trusted to trained men. If it wishes for light upon that awful matter, it asks men who know no more law than I know, but who can feel the things that I felt in the jury box. When it wants a library cataloged, or the solar system discovered, or any trifle of that kind, it uses up its specialists. But when it wishes anything done which is really serious, it collects twelve of the ordinary men standing round. The same thing was done if I remember right, by the Founder of Christianity.[1]

There are certainly times where juries get it wrong—they are, after all, made up of humans. Over time, various rules and structures have evolved that better insure valid jury results, and the simple truth is that the American judicial system, when it is working right and under its rules, remains a bulwark for citizens' rights and for determining historical facts behind differing claims. The jury's decision is so sacrosanct that the US Constitution and Bill of Rights ensures that it is not even open to reexamination absent some minor exceptions.

In making this "jury argument" on the existence of God, I want to organize my approach into several areas that need to be addressed and understood individually before drawing a final conclusion.

THE BURDEN OF PROOF

One of the keys to a jury's decision is the basis on which a jury is instructed to find truth. I was discussing this point recently while fishing with a United States Supreme Court judge. We were joined in the boat by a guide who maneuvered us artfully through the Louisiana waters in search of dinner. As the day wore on, our discussion turned to the issue of why we believe in God. The justice, a well-educated man who is brilliant—plain and simple—is a devout Christian believer. I suggested to him that framing the deliberation process before framing the question is of paramount importance. Here is what I mean.

There are many valid units of measurement. Gallons and quarts (or liters if we use the metric system) measure liquids. Inches, feet, yards, meters, kilometers and miles express distance. Fahrenheit and centigrade scales measure temperature. Each term works to measure its category, but not matters outside its category. While I can validly measure the heat outside as 72 degrees Fahrenheit (or 22 degrees Celsius), I would never say the temperature is 6 gallons. Conversely, if I were discussing how much gas I put in my car, I might say 6 gallons, but never 72 degrees Fahrenheit. We must be careful to use the right measuring system for the category or item being measured.

In the same way, we err in any discussion of the existence of God if we use the wrong measure of proof. It is as absurd to think of proving God in the scientific sense of a lab process or the mathematical precision of a calculator as it is to measure distance by gallons. Ultimate questions like God's existence call for an appropriate measurement of proof. I suggest the measurement of proof from the American jury system.

History has fine-tuned our jury trials to efficiently and fairly determine truth. It is done in civil cases by a "preponderance of the evidence" burden of proof. This means that before a jury can find for the party that carries the "burden of proof," the jury must be persuaded by the "greater weight of the credible evidence." This is also defined as "What is more likely than not?"

This is the appropriate measurement for truth, and it is my suggestion for our consideration of the existence of God. We should no more seek scientific proof of God than we seek to determine time by kilograms and pounds. The proper measure of proof is to ask simply: What is more reasonable to believe—that there is a God or that there is not? With that burden of proof set out, we move into the direct question under consideration.

DIALOGUE WITH THE GOLDEN RULE ATHEIST

Mike, sitting to my right, was a lawyer who had initially studied for the priesthood, but that was before he lost his faith. Now he was a middle-aged man who proclaimed to our group, "I am a golden rule atheist." He explained that he believed in the golden rule, but not the God who taught it. I asked him what he understood the golden rule to be. He responded properly, "To do to others what you would like for others to do to you." I was intrigued.

Although he didn't realize it, he was displaying classic circumstances that are proof for the reality of God. It was my task to try to show him.

"Why on earth would you believe in or live by the golden rule?" I asked.

He replied that he thought it was the way of the world and inherent in nature.

I was a bit incredulous and replied, "I am stunned! Do you really think so? Or does this just sound like a noble and nice thing to say?"

He replied that he wasn't saying it to sound noble, but that it is the way of civilization and life.

"But don't you believe in evolution?" I asked.

"Yes," he replied as a few others in the group began to realize where I was going.

I hit the pointed question: "Are you actually believing that Darwinism and evolution brought about humans because animals were treating others the way they would like to be treated? For that matter, does the history of the human race indicate it is the normative behavior for people groups?"

As we worked through it, he had to admit that animals have not embraced that motto or ethic. The lion that separates the young gazelle from its mother in order to devour its flesh is not treating that young gazelle the way the lion would like to be treated. For that matter, Mike himself was no vegan, readily devouring the steak just served for dinner.

Mike then shifted his position to the idea that human consciousness makes this a new ethic that did not exist in the universe for its first few billion years but has cropped up in the last few millennia of human civilization. Where it came from, Mike couldn't say. How he knew it was valid, Mike couldn't say. Why it suddenly appeared, Mike couldn't say. Would it be here to stay, Mike couldn't say. One thing Mike could say—he didn't live up to his ethic.

As much as Mike believed it was right, he readily admitted he saw it as an ideal, not as something he was able to do day by day, minute by minute. It was something Mike internally felt was right and proper, even though it was unachievable.

My suggestion to Mike was that he needed to give the most reasonable explanation for why this was such a core belief to him. Recognizing it was something apparently unique to humans, he had to make some choices about why.

While Mike didn't have an immediate response, if he had time to consider it, he might have argued that the golden rule is a uniquely human ethic or trait because humanity has a brain that enables empathy, while other creatures do not. In other words, humans can think about what it would be like to be in another's shoes. From this ability to empathize comes a responsibility to empathize. But even with that response, I would have pushed him further. That ability to empathize does not mean a responsibility to do so in the sense of the golden rule. That is not a fair deduction.

The lawyer in me would declare, "Objection! This is akin to post hoc ergo propter hoc." In other words, just because one event precedes another, it does not mean that the first event caused the second. Just because people developed a brain that can empathize does not mean that people have a responsibility to treat others as they would like to be treated.

The ability to empathize could also be seen as a weapon to be used to help one advance over others. There is inherent in most people, to some degree or another, a competitive streak. Few really like to lose. Perhaps empathy is a tool to help us imagine another's thoughts so we can anticipate actions. This would be key to winning in the game of life. Any chess player would tell you their winning odds go way up if they know what moves their opponent will make before the moves are executed.

Mike's recognition of a morality he is unable to live up to is in fact an indicator that there is something beyond Mike, and beyond the universe, that is prescribing right and wrong.

DIALOGUE WITH THE NONVEGAN VEGAN

I moved my discussion with Mike to another subject.

"Did you eat your steak?" I asked, having just finished our dinner.

"Of course! And it was great!" he replied.

I looked surprised as I asked, "Wow! Don't you feel guilty?"

He knew I was headed somewhere, but didn't know where yet.

"No, why should I feel guilty?"

"Because," I replied, "You have eaten another living being. Would you eat your grandmother?"

"Of course not," he replied, appropriately.

I said, "But I thought you lived by the golden rule. Surely you wouldn't want to be bred and eaten for dinner?"

"Oh," he replied, "The golden rule just counts for people."

"But don't you believe that people are just another form of animals? How about some old person you don't know. Would you willingly eat them?"

"Never!" he answered.

"Why not?" I asked, wanting a real answer. "After all, you believe that people are just the same energy and matter collected in a different form than the energy and matter collected in a cow."

"Well, for one . . ." he answered, thinking it through as it was slowly coming out of his mouth, "people have consciousness different than a cow."

I pushed further, "So if someone is in the hospital brain dead, with no hope of ever resuscitating, you would have no problem eating such a one, or feeding the comatose person to one who is starving and in need of nourishing protein?"

No, he wasn't okay with that either.

I pointed out to him that he seemed to give some greater significance to the collection of atoms and energy we call "people" as opposed to any other collection of matter and energy. He had no real reasonable explanation beyond the idea of human nobility, but why that dignity for a human should be there, Mike didn't know.

My suggestion, of course, was that we were looking at another way that Mike's life and his core beliefs were actually aligned with the idea that there is a God who has made humans special ("in his image" is the biblical phrase) and hence different from all other animals. Of course, without a God there is no "image," and the uniqueness that flows from that is gone. This is circumstantial evidence.

DIALOGUE WITH THE OBJECTIVE SUBJECTIVIST

Objective and *subjective* are two very critical words in any trial or any discussion of truth. *Objective* means that something outside of a person is involved in defining or making a truth. *Subjective* means that the truth proceeds from a person or a subject. Here are two examples.

- If a witness offers objective testimony that John died of a heart attack, the witness might refer to an autopsy that showed myocardial infarction, with not only heart tissue death from oxygen deprivation but also the presence of a clot in the appropriate vessel. In other words, there was an objective finding upon autopsy that showed the heart attack.

- If a witness offers subjective testimony on whether John died of a heart attack, the witness might say she or he felt that John was a likely candidate for a heart attack and, even though he or she does not know for certain, thinks it's the reason that John fell down dead.

A judge would allow the objective evidence into trial. The judge would not, absent some other reason, allow the subjective opinion of John's death into trial. There is no legitimate basis in the subjective opinion to let it into evidence. One person's opinion is little better than another's.

"Objective" and "subjective" were also important ideas in the conversation I was having with Mike and others in our small discussion group. For Mike, the golden rule was his core ethic. Not so for the others.

One in our group was quick to point out that the golden rule was not his guiding principle, nor should it be. His point was that we are in a competitive, dog-eat-dog world, and the goal is to be the one on top. He would not run roughshod over people, but his clear intent is to die with the most toys. His moral compass is pointed to self-interest, not the betterment of society.

Now lest we think him callous, he might rejoin that capitalism is built on his ethic, not on the golden rule. The desire to capitalize on one's own industriousness and self-interest propelled Western civilization, and certainly America, into a global leadership position in technology, inventions and productivity. We want more money to buy more things, and so we work to get that money. We may want more money to acquire security or prestige rather than chattels (a legal word for personal property), but we are still seeking things for ourselves.

Here is where Mike's dilemma lies. Mike wants an objective ethic, he wants his rule of right and wrong to be more than a concoction of his head or noble desire of his heart. In fact, every fiber in his being shouts that there is an objective right and wrong. As Mike kept reiterating to me, "I don't know why it's right, but it is!"

Mike has no basis for such an objective view. Without God or some other outside objective source for right and wrong, Mike is stuck with an ethic that is his, but only out of choice—not because of its inherent truth as an ideal or what is truly right.

Even those who believed in a dog-eat-dog world gave strong circumstantial proof for God. I asked them if they would mind terribly if I took some of their "stuff" when they weren't looking. All replied, "Well of course! That would be stealing!"

"And is stealing wrong, or is it merely offensive?"

They all believed stealing was wrong.

I pushed them further, "Well, what you are saying is, it is wrong for you to be stolen from because you don't like it. But you'd agree it is right for me to steal since this is a dog-eat-dog world and I want your stuff!"

No, they would not go there with me. This was a sticking point where their inner convictions were circumstantial evidence that something outside them was dictating right and wrong. There was an objective morality that eclipsed their worldview.

Since we were all lawyers, it is surprising no one said, "But that's illegal!" Of course, they may have realized "being legal" does not equate with "being right." Slavery was legal, but it wasn't right. Hitler's actions were legal, but no one would agree with them.

DIALOGUE ON CREATION VERSUS EVOLUTION

Nick propelled our discussion into something a bit more concrete— creation or evolution. His request was simple, "How do you square the truth you know with Genesis? Do you expect us to believe in Adam and Eve? How can you write off all the proof of evolution?"

I loved his question, and told him so! The lawyer in me, however, would have to file two objections to the question as phrased. First, it is "multifarious." By that I mean that the two questions are distinct and need to be addressed separately. Second, the questions "assume facts not in evidence." Here is how I explained my answer, along with the objections.

"Nick, what if I were to tell you that one can read Genesis faithfully to its message and not engage the evolution question one way or the other?"

"What do you mean?" he asked.

I told him that I believed Genesis to be true, but that Nick and others are reading it for a truth that is not necessarily in the text. The text is not written for science; it is written for significance. Science is really a product of the last five hundred years. It was not the concern of the Israelites living in the midst of pagan tribes and nations over three thousand years ago. Before we read the Bible from our current perspective, we need to read it from the ancient perspective. If I say "7 up" I might refer to a drink, to a score or to a number that is next in line. It all depends on context. Often that context is historical.

Before asking what Genesis says to us today, we have a responsibility to ask what Genesis said to those Israelites to whom it was first written. Genesis told the Israelites that creation was not what their neighbors thought, either as it reflected the value and role of people or in its reflection on the presence and nature of God.

As a witness here, we can call to the stand Assyrian king Ashurbanipal. Over twenty-five hundred years ago he maintained a tremendous library with thousands of clay tablets. Those tablets covered most every subject, from the mundane to the fanciful (legal tablets, transactional tablets, etc.). Of course, the king died, his empire crumbled and time overcame his library, burying the building and its contents.

But Ashurbanipal ruled in a hot, dry capital city named Nineveh. The weather was perfect for preserving the clay tablets. So when, in the mid-1800s, archaeologists discovered these tablets, the ancient stories were found, and scholarship of the Old Testament has never been the same.

Two of the important ancient Mesopotamian stories found in clay cuneiform tablets are called the *Atrahasis* and the *Enuma Elish*. In these stories we read how Israel's neighbors thought that the gods were created. After being created the gods' first efforts were to fight chaos and bring order to the world. As the gods continued to multiply, they did all sorts of human things, though on a grander, more godlike scale. There were working gods who dug the Tigris and Euphrates rivers, piling up the dirt into mountains. There were warring gods, who fought against each other, hacking one dead goddess into two and hurling half of her body into the sky to form the dome of heaven.

In these stories the gods possessed aspects of creation they either made or came to own. So the god who owned the storms had jurisdiction and control over the weather. The god who owned the sea was the sea. The god who possessed a certain area of the earth could be both in that earth and also presiding over that part of earth.

Those stories also explained an origin of people. Men and women were made to take burdens off the gods. The gods' chores were hard work. It started to wear on them, and they decided to make people so people could finish the chores of the gods.

Radically, into cultures built from these ideologies came the Bible creation story, one that is as opposite as possible. In the Bible there is one God, not many. God is not made; he is the maker. God does not war against chaos in an effort to bring order; God creates the world in an orderly fashion, forming and filling it in ways that are "very good." God does not simply make one aspect of creation to inhabit and rule over; he makes all of creation. He makes everything. God is not relegated to a certain piece of real estate; he presides over all there is. Creation is not a part of God or an aspect of his body. Creation is independent of God, something he spoke into being.

Unlike the neighboring stories, God did not grow weary from creating. He was not challenged in digging creeks and rivers or in building mountains. God made all with his words. He rested not out of fatigue but because his work was finished, and it was "very good"! Human beings were not made to relieve God of burdens; we were made in God's image to enjoy his fellowship and company.

The historical context view sees the Genesis account as setting out the truth of God and his creation, not in the sense of science and history, but as a story that taught a competing reality to other creation stories.

Now there are more intricate discussions to be had on Genesis, but for my purposes with Nick this was a sufficient starting point. It allowed me to move past the issue of whether Genesis or evolution was right. It also allowed me to propose a scientific question to him, "Exactly where do you think the subject matter for the Big Bang came from?"

He replied there were a number of theories on this. I agreed; I had read and considered those, but my question for him was which one he found more reasonable than that a God created it.

"Maybe it just was always there!"

I asked him his basis for that belief. Where has he ever seen anything that suggests something can just be? That involves quite a leap of faith. Of course, he could argue the same might be said for the belief in God. But there is a ready answer at my disposal that Nick is missing. The idea of God existing outside of space and time means that beginning and end is no longer a question or issue. Time itself is a creation, not something that has always been and always will be. Now in terms of the universe, time is irrevocably interwoven in to the warp and woof of space and matter. But the idea of a God outside the space-time continuum is exactly that—a God outside of time.

The discussion then moved from creation versus evolution to Nick's second question.

DIALOGUES ON ADAM AND EVE

Nick's question to me included an argument for Adam and Eve. As he worded it, "How can you believe there was one woman and one man?" This is an interesting question. Look at it carefully. How can you believe there was one man and one woman? Shall we say, as opposed to two? Three? One hundred?

I came from one man and one woman. They are my parents—Mom

and Dad. Each of them came from one man and one woman—my grandparents. Each of those came from one man and one woman. I daresay we have not even a hint in our lineage that anyone came from more than one man and one woman!

How does that go back in history? Current statistics indicate a world population of roughly 7.1 billion people. Scholars generally accord that the population has grown continuously since the Great Famine and Black Death in 1350. Then the population stood around 370 million.[2] Going back historically from there, it is more difficult to assign population numbers with precision. Still, at some point, the population will go back to a mother and father, even among the evolution believers.

There is genetic evidence that the first evolved modern people were so closely related genetically to alternate primate species that there was interbreeding, but even that would source to a single mother.

The biblical teaching that modern women and men are direct descendants of a man and woman is not any more far-fetched than the idea posed by evolution. To me, these are issues worthy of discussion, but they are not issues that get to the existence or nonexistence of God. Therefore, even though I would have loved to have discussed them with Nick, they are readily subject to the lawyer's cry, "Objection, relevance." These issues are not relevant to whether there is a God, except for one aspect. The biblical account teaches us a profundity of humanity that helps explain much of our earlier discussion. This is the lesson of Genesis that I next discussed with my friends.

THE SIGNIFICANCE OF THE BIBLICAL ACCOUNT

Nick's challenge for me to square reality with Genesis hinged on an important point. My question was simple, "Do you want me to square Genesis with what it says or with what you think it says?"

Those two I knew to be vastly different.

I told Nick I would do two things with Genesis. First, I would square Genesis with what it actually says, not what Nick thought it said. Second, I would square Genesis with reality. Genesis is my source to make sense of the world as Nick, Mike, me or anyone else experiences it. Genesis makes sense with the circumstantial evidence of life.

Most anyone reading the ancient pagan creation accounts would be immediately struck by the uniqueness of Genesis. If we are reading Genesis for ideas contained in the accounts, we come away with several noteworthy points that argue for a certain perspective of God, the world and humanity. These points are quite distinct from the views of Israel's neighbors. This is important as I give the argument that concludes this chapter.

One God versus many. The first and obvious difference between the Bible and the religious documents of other ancient neighbors to Israel concerns the number of gods. Rather than believing in many deities (some systems had hundreds of gods), Genesis taught Israel that there is only one. In Genesis, one God creates everything: heavens, earth, sky, seas, land, vegetation, sun, moon, stars, animals and people. There are not gods for each item or area. There is no competition between gods. The one God is over all of nature. He controls everything.

God is above creation, not a part of creation. Another notable point in the Genesis account is the transcendence of God. As the God who existed before any creation, and as the God who does the actual creating, the Bible's God is apart from the things created. In a sense, God is the *supernature*, the one beyond and outside of the natural order, from which we derive the term *supernatural*.

We must note how different this was from Israel's neighbors. For many of the neighbors, the gods themselves were the sky, the moon, the sun and so on (or at least they were inextricably linked to those elements of nature). If you were to go to Egypt and look at the ceiling of a monument built by or for Pharaoh Seti I (ruled from c. 1291–1279 B.C.) called the Osirion, then you would see the engraved story of a goddess called Nut. Nut was stretched out above the atmosphere as the sky. Another god, Shu (who was the atmosphere), held up Nut. Shu in turn stood on Geb, the god of the earth. Other gods, including the sun, moon and stars, would come forth from various parts of Nut and then return at their appropriate times. Shu was not only holding up Nut, but with the help of another four to eight gods Shu also held back the waters in the heavens.

Not so with God as revealed in the Bible. He is not found in the sun or in a nearby storm. God is beyond and controls creation. *God is outside space-time, not captive to space-time.* When we speak of space and time, we are using modern scientific ideas and words. However, the gist of those concepts is a valid way to verbalize a difference in understanding that came from Israel's revelation.

A singular God who reigns over all nature, whether in space or time, is not subject to the laws of nature. This is a miracle-working God who can bend, suspend or alter things by the mere word of his mouth. An over-age couple has a baby, dreams have meaning, famine is foreseen, bushes burn without getting burned up, seas are parted and people are delivered—all of which we read about in the later pages of the books of Genesis and Exodus.

In contrast, in the Babylonian epic *Enuma Elish* we read of the main god (Apsu) being put to sleep through a magical spell cast by Ea, his offspring. While asleep, Apsu is tied up and killed. The God of the Bible is not so vulnerable. God is above creation, neither a part of it nor subject to it. In the Bible account God reveals himself to be beyond the material world and its time. God made time (morning and evening, day one, etc.); he is not subject to time.

God is not a sexual being. As Israel's neighbors went about constructing images of the gods, they conceived of the gods as they did all other beings—male and female—not like the unique God we find in the Bible. The writings of Israel's neighbors proclaim how the gods were made. In the *Enuma Elish*, Apsu and Tiamat "were mingling their waters together" when "the gods were formed between them."

A reading of the Hittite legends includes sordid tales of physical and sexual conquests among the gods that affect their interactions with creation. In *Elkunirsa and Asertu* we read of the god El (creator of earth) and his goddess wife, Asertu. Without El's knowledge, Asertu attempts to seduce the god Ba'al, who refuses her advances. Asertu then complains to her husband, and we read about the gods plotting and scheming behind each other's backs in a divine saga that reads like a lurid soap opera. This is not what is taught in the Bible. Genesis teaches that God made humanity in his image, both "male and female" (Gen 1:27). As such, God is neither male nor female, but both sexes find themselves expressing some aspects of God.

God does not have human limitations. God is not a human in supersized form. God does not have limitations of strength, drive or emotions. This sets apart the God of Genesis from the gods of Israel's contemporaries.

Contrast the gods in the *Enuma Elish*. A point was reached when the younger gods were bothersome to the older gods because of their "offensive behavior" and their "noisome actions." The older god Apsu yelled at his wife (mother of the younger gods): "Their behavior is noisome to me! By day I have no rest, at night I do not sleep! I wish to put an end to their behavior, to do away with it! Let silence reign that we may sleep!"

With that, the gods started plotting to kill each other. After the killing starts, war is brought on for some time until a peaceful accord is reached. As we continue to read the story, we see more limitations of the gods. A principle victor in the *Enuma Elish* is the god Marduk, who also decided to create humans. His reason? The gods were tired from their hard work! People were made to "bear the gods' burden that those [the gods] may rest."[3]

Similarly in the *Atrahasis*, people were made because the gods

did forced labor . . . digging watercourses. . . . They heaped up all the mountains. . . . Forced labor they bore night and day. [They were com]plaining, denouncing, [mut]tering down in the ditch . . . [the gods then say], "Let the midwife create a human being, Let man assume the drudgery of god."[4]

These gods also pouted. In a Hittite story one god named Telipinu gets angry, leaves his job post and goes to sleep in a meadow. To understand the significance of this to the people, we must realize that

In the Hittite view, the operation of the universe required that each deity and human conscientiously perform his or her proper function within the whole. Calamity manifested in some sector of the cosmos was an indication that the god or goddess responsible for it had become angry and had abandoned his or her post.[5]

Once Telipinu leaves, the world falls apart! Breeding of livestock stops, the weather goes haywire, famine hits the land and crops will not grow, and even the gods themselves cannot eat a satisfying meal. The Storm god (Telipinu's father) does not know where his son is and refuses to look for him in spite of his wife's (the Mother goddess) vehement demands. So, the Mother goddess sends a bee to find her son.

The bee finds the god and stings him a few times to wake him up, which only increases his anger. At that point everyone (human and divine) goes to work to get Telipinu in a better mood and restore order to the world.

Into these cultures comes the Bible's revelation of God as the Creator. God is not a larger version of a human. He has none of the human foibles. In fact, humanity itself has none of those foibles until sin enters the picture.

Creation was not hard work for God. He spoke and it came to be. At the end of six days of creation, there was a day of rest, but the text gives no indication that God was fatigued on the seventh day. Instead, the sabbath's "rest" was simply the end of creative activity.

Sabbath is our English version of the Hebrew word formed from the root *shbt*. The verb in its root means "to cease." On the seventh day God quit working because his work was finished. God had made a world that was very good.

Regarding tiresome work, in making humans the gods of neighboring cultures had much work to do. They had to kill a god for the necessary blood to mix with clay. Needless to say, figuring out which god to kill and then killing that god was no simple matter. In Genesis we see the contrast of God speaking everything into existence. Adam was fashioned out of the dust of the field; no god died. God simply breathed life into Adam.

God stands out as the authority over all there is. All of Scripture begins with the declaration "In the beginning, God created the heavens and the earth" (Gen 1:1). When the earth was formless and void, God spoke and it was both formed and filled. God does not fight with his counsel in his creation; he speaks his plans, "Let us . . . ," and the plans come to fruition. God has no human limitations.

Nature's role with humankind. Where the Genesis creation account stands out from the secular versions is in the makeup and the function of nature. The makeup we discussed earlier. For most

of Israel's neighbors, these celestial features were actually associated
with individual gods. In Genesis nature is simply creation. The elements are not of God or in God; God made the elements. Beyond
that, Genesis teaches the unique function of the created elements.
For Israel's neighbors, the cosmos contained elements tamed by the
gods and then used for the gods' purposes. People were made to
work the earth to the benefit of the gods. Genesis sets the story the
other way around.

In Genesis, God makes the cosmos for people. God forms heaven,
earth, sky and seas, filling them with fish, birds and animals. Each
creature is to produce more after its own kind. People would have
stewardship and dominion over all creatures, and the creatures
would serve humanity, not God (Gen 1:26). God makes plants as
food for beasts, but ultimately for people (Gen 1:29). God creates
the sun and stars, but does so not for himself but to establish
seasons for people (Gen 1:14).

Genesis's teaching on men and women. The revelation of man and
woman and their purpose and role is likewise different than that of
Israel's neighbors. Genesis speaks clearly of two people as the pro-
genitors of the entire human race; the other creation accounts have
the gods making people in groups.

Unlike Genesis, a number of ancient accounts have the creating
deities mixing physical elements of the gods (tears, flesh, blood,
etc.) with clay to make humans. This shows the connection between humans and deities. In Genesis, however, the connection is
by the breath (spirit) that God provides to people as he makes them
in his image. This gives Adam and Eve a unique relational connection with the Creator.

Genesis says that people are made in God's "image" (Gen 1:26-
27). This is not a physical image. Rather, the image implies responsibility and identity of role and function. In other words,

people had the responsibilities God assigned as well as the abilities necessary to accomplish the tasks. This has a number of implications.

People have the ability to create, to think, to choose, to plan, to accomplish, to appreciate, to discern, to process and to communicate. These are abilities that God possesses and dispensed to all humans. In Genesis, humans are given the necessary qualities of God to do his work on his behalf as his representatives. The implications for human value are paramount. Our value lies in the imprint of God's image. Our true value is not in looks, brains, social position, physical dexterity or athletic talent. Our value is in our nature as an image bearer of the almighty Creator God.

The Genesis teaching on the effects of the fall. Genesis teaches that God made things "very good" (Gen 1:31). But after God's good work was finished, humans took control and did things contrary to the will and nature of God. By so doing Adam and Eve lost the intimate fellowship they enjoyed with God and subsequently lived in rebellion, with all of its consequences, including nature fighting against human survival rather than aiding it. As Genesis puts it, Adam now had to toil among thorns and thistles to eke out a living. Birthing children would be painful to Eve, not simply a blessing of life.

The world is not as God created it. This leaves us, according to Genesis, living with struggles and stress, always inherently knowing there could be so much more. We cry out against injustice. We recognize, or at least hope, that life should have some kind of meaning. We dream of a situation more beautiful or better than we presently have, and we work toward it, as if we were made for it.

This is strong circumstantial evidence of God. This human experience is explained in the Genesis story. It is rooted in who we are and who we were made to be.

THE POINT

One of the things I always look for in any argument is consistency. Does an argument have internal consistency? Can a position be tested and measured against other beliefs to determine consistency? This is important in direct evidence, but it is critically important when assessing circumstantial evidence.

I might say that I believe that team A is the best football team in the world, but if I look at its win-loss record and find it abysmal, I have a consistency issue between my belief and reality. Now maybe there are reasons reality is inconsistent with my beliefs, and perhaps my beliefs are right in spite of reality, but the odds are quite low. It is more reasonable that reality needs to correct my opinion.

So it is with life. Mike, Nick and others want to believe there is no God. They want to embrace a world and life that has nothing beyond humanity as its ultimate significance. Yet I beg for a reality check. Do they live consistent with this perception? How can Mike be a golden rule atheist? His belief reflects a truth in morality that is difficult to square with his atheism.

Both Nick and Mike, and many other atheists and agnostics, hold to ideas and values that argue for a source beyond themselves. We don't eat other humans, because humans are special. This works from the biblical perspective, but not so well from Mike's and Nick's.

The twentieth-century Oxford and Cambridge scholar C. S. Lewis was an atheist during his early adult life. From there he became a theist, believing in God but not necessarily the Christian God. Finally, he became a believing Christian. In his essay "Is Theology Poetry?" Lewis wrote, "I believe in Christianity as I believe that the sun has risen: not only because I see it, but because by it I see everything else."[6] Lewis makes a compelling point. Even the most ardent atheist or agnostic, on close examination, will find their lives reflecting the world with a God and the values imparted by God. The inconsistency of life and belief is a compelling reason to grant the existence of a God. At least to this lawyer, it seems the more reasonable likelihood. It better represents the reality I see day to day.

Now who might this God be? Well, that is an examination that begins in chapter three!

3

Who God Is Not!

COURTROOMS ARE OMINOUS PLACES. All rise as the judge enters and the court is called to order. The judge wears black robes and carries immense authority.

When you are in trial, a judge tells you what time to be at court, how long you stay at court, when you can speak, when you must listen, when you can eat and when you can go to the restroom. The judge has an ability to make your life comfortable or quite difficult.

Lawyers rate judges. I was recently asked to give a speech to a collection of five hundred judges. My assigned topic was "What Makes a Gold Medal Judge?" I was asked to parse through characteristics that make a judge bad or good.

As I prepared for the speech, I went through my past experiences. My view of gold medal judges was shaped by my exposure over almost three decades of trying cases from coast to coast. Many judges were good, a few were truly great, and regarding some I would rather take a beating than be in front of them again.

My goal was to influence those judges listening so they might better discharge their responsibilities as officers of the court. They could hear my tales and decide which type of judge they wanted to be. They may never know some of the judges I was referencing, but hearing my reflections might influence them nonetheless.

Our views of the God of the Bible are not always shaped by firsthand experience. Many people carry a view of God that is more reflective of what they have been told, what they have read, even what they have seen on television. Few people take time to read the Bible carefully to determine what is revealed and claimed about God.

As I lectured on judicial temperament and behavior, I had two goals in mind. First, I wanted to identify negative behavior and views that produce a less than desirable judge. Then I wanted to give the positives. I wanted to explain what traits were admirable and laudable.

Similarly, it is important to use a dual approach to studying the biblical God. Especially when so many people carry secondhand views about God, we must first identify who God is not. This identifies and removes nonbiblical views of God that may have snuck into our brains, even though disguised as valid. This is my goal in this chapter. Then I will use the two following chapters to affirm teachings about God found in the Bible and Christian faith.

We want our examination in this book to be of the Christian God, not some other idea.

Witness List

John Bertram (J. B.) Phillips (1906–1982). *J. B. Phillips was an Anglican clergyman, author and Bible translator. He sought to translate God and the Bible into the relevant language of his day. During World War II he decided that most young people could not understand the King James Bible. So from a bomb shelter he began translating the New Testament. After the war Phillips noticed that the populace had a poor perception of God, not seeing him as relevant to the new, huge problems of a nuclear age. Phillips addressed this in a book,* Your God Is Too Small. *Both Phillips's Bible translation and his book are popular sellers today.*

The biblical concept and teaching about God are distinct from the views of God that many associate with Christianity. There is not one section of the Bible that sets out "All You Need to Know to Understand God Rightly." The Bible reveals God through stories, narratives, interactions, legal proclamations, prophetic declarations and in the life of Jesus Christ. The picture is both complex and simple at the same time. Further, the Bible teaches that God can be known truly, but not fully. No one can comprehend God in his glory. We are not remotely up to such a task.

As a result, many people live with an understanding or belief in God that seems more rooted in common experience than in sound theology. False views of God easily creep into our lives—they are how we think God should be, rather than from the biblical revelation of who he is. In this chapter we consider some of these concepts of God, many of which are held by people who profess the Christian faith.

We begin our examination of "who God is not" by calling to the stand J. B. Phillips.

In 1952 British clergyman J. B. Phillips published the Christian classic *Your God Is Too Small*.[1] This masterpiece was penned both to grow Christian believers and to aid the skeptic. Phillips wrote at a time when the world was upside down. Just seven years earlier the world finished a devastating war and unveiled an attempted genocide of the Jewish people. Science gave the world two exploded atomic bombs, bursting humanity into the nuclear age. Splitting the atom changed the profile of war and armed conflict in ways that threatened every nation and even humanity itself.

In the midst of those major changes Phillips found that the average person's mental horizons had "expanded to the point of bewilderment by world events and by scientific discoveries." Many people were without "a God big enough for modern needs."[2]

Phillips wrote to educate, to instill faith and to encourage people living in a new age to better understand God. We can use Phillips's testimony to set out common misperceptions of God, hoping to identify and remove inadequate and unbiblical images of God before examining the more biblical views. I will use many of Phillips's categories, modified and updated as appropriate, as we consider his testimony of who or what God is not before then calling witnesses to what or who God is.

FALSE VIEWS OF GOD

A morality cop. Some people wrongly equate God with their consciences, making God a morality cop. They perceive God as that voice inside that approves of good and disapproves of bad choices. He is internal affirmation or guilt. Such a view of God might be affirming in many ways, but that neither makes it a biblical nor a logical view of God.

Common sense shows that no one's conscience is an infallible guide. In fact, what violates one person's conscience might be affirmed in another's, depending on their upbringing. Even in my own lifetime I have seen my conscience change, modify and grow on some matters. I suspect most people have.

Does that mean that God changed or that morality changed? Of course not. It is part of learning and maturing. The conscience can also be altered by brainwashing, poor education and other indoctrinations. Atrocities like the 9/11 attacks illustrate the perversion of the conscience. Those terrorists likely believed their actions were appropriate, even holy. All they really showed was how deluded one's conscience can become.

A supersized earthly father. People might believe God is a supersized father perhaps because in the New Testament he is repeatedly called Father. The New Testament is centered on Jesus of Nazareth,

proclaimed in those pages as the unique Son of God. Jesus described God as "our Father in heaven." If we stop there, we might
walk away thinking of God as a supersized human father, but Jesus
was not insinuating that God is merely a super-human. We must be
wary of thinking that God is a human on a grander scale.

Jesus' truth about God includes the fact that he cares for us in a
special way. But no one has ever had a perfect father, and God is not
subjected to the shortcomings of our earthly fathers. The biblical
analogy of God as Father is meant to illustrate that God has an
intimate love for and interest in his people, just as a good father
does for his children. But some people have grown up with angry,
tyrannical, indulgent or unjust fathers, and *they* must be extra
careful in thinking of God as Father. This might cause an image of
God as a fearful being who is both unapproachable and difficult to
worship. God is no such father.

There is a second concern when considering God as a bigger-
than-life earthly father. Some secular psychologists teach that a
Christian belief in God is rooted in a person's regressive desire to
be a dependent child clinging to a parent. This is not a valid biblical
concept of God. The biblical God is seeking to grow his children
mentally, emotionally and spiritually. Paul (aka "Saul of Tarsus"), a
first-century church planter and author of multiple letters in the
New Testament, urged his readers to grow into the solid food of
spiritual maturity, not the milk of spiritual babies (1 Cor 3:1-4). He
told the church at Rome that growing in God includes renewing
their minds (Rom 12:1-2).

Some might object, noting that Jesus called his disciples to
"become like children" (Mt 18:1-3). But Jesus was not calling his
disciples to immaturity. He wanted them to walk in the humility
of a child rather than the arrogance of many adults. He wanted
them to repudiate the sham, the compromise and the cynicism

of adulthood. It was not an instruction to romp around in spiritual diapers.

The old man in the sky. For some people God is an old man sitting in a heavenly rocking chair watching events unfold on earth and periodically dabbling in people's affairs. Some think God was much more likely to do this in days gone by, almost unconsciously perceiving that he was more active in his youth. Perhaps this is traceable to the idea that as we were growing, we saw our superiors as old. Thus, God, the ultimate superior one, is some old gentleman in heaven. Damage from this view includes the tendency to view God as not simply aged but also old-fashioned, with inadequate energy and contemporary awareness to operate satisfactorily in the complexities of present or future.

Once this view is placed front and center, however, the absurdity of it becomes obvious. God is called by Daniel the "Ancient of Days," but that should never be construed to mean that he is out of date. The Bible shows God as the God of history, of the atomic age and of any age to come. God makes contemporary seem out of date.

The Force. When *Star Wars* hit the cinema screen in 1977, pop culture was introduced to the "Force," a godlike power that coursed through the universe performing otherwise impossible tasks through people especially tuned to it. In the first film we were told the Force is an energy field created by all living things. This field surrounds everyone and supposedly holds the galaxy together. As a life force it has both a dark and a light side, and people use both aspects of the Force in the struggle of good versus bad. In later films the ideas of the Force continued to develop with monastic orders of priests.

This idea of a force was not simply an ingenious creation of George Lucas. It was fashioned from an idea of cinematographer Roman Kriotor, who in an earlier film much studied by Lucas said,

"Many people feel that in the contemplation of nature and in communication with other living things, they become aware of some kind of force, or something, behind this apparent mask which we see in front of us, and they call it God."[3]

Lucas called this idea simply the Force, adding in an interview, "Similar phrases have been used extensively by many different people for the last 13,000 years to describe the 'life force.'"[4]

The Force is not the view of God given in the Bible, however. The God of the Bible is a distinct being, the Creator of life, not the reflection or assimilation of it. The God of the Bible has existence totally apart from the universe and any life contained in it. Theologians refer to this as the *transcendence* of God, in the sense that he transcends matter and the natural order. In the following chapters we will explore whether this idea of God as both personal and transcendent is reasonable.

The God of many paths. Through film and book many people grew to love Piscine Molitor Patel, a young man from Pondicherry, India, who went by the nickname Pi. In *Life of Pi* we read of Pi growing up a Hindu, but studying Christianity and Islam, and at age fourteen deciding to embrace all three religions simultaneously. For Pi each religion has its strengths, and he sees each as a revelation that helps him find his path to the divine.

Many people today consider the God of the Bible one of many excellent choices for finding the divine and for finding meaning in life. Yet is that a fair rendition of the God of the Bible? Do many paths lead not only to meaning and purpose but to the truth of what lies beyond? The Bible makes strong claims to a distinctiveness that denies the idea of many roads to God. Early on, in the first of the Ten Commandments, God says, "I am the LORD your God. . . . You shall have no other gods before me. . . . You shall not bow down to them or serve them, for I the LORD your God am a jealous God"

(Ex 20:2-3, 5). We will examine and test the reasonableness of this claim in the coming chapters.

God of strict perfection. The Bible clearly teaches that God is perfect. The God of strict perfection view is not about this but believes that God requires perfection in his children. Contrary to this view, the Bible teaches that God gave an ultimate expression of his love for people at a time when they were mired in sin.

If we think we have to *achieve* personal perfection, we are in bad shape. It will either lead to guilt and misery, or we may cheapen the standard of perfection and wrongly think we have reached it. Either way we will be mired in guilt or proud arrogance, both of which are destructive. This view fails to appreciate that God is at work in his people to bring us closer to perfection, even though perfection is not achieved in this life.

The escape God. The escape God makes religious faith a form of psychological escapism. God, in this view, provides an escape from the storms and stresses of life. Like many of these views, it has an element of truth, but it is not the full truth of the God of the Bible. Sadly, this view allows one to stay in a state of emotional immaturity and childish regression.

> Those who are actually, though unconsciously, looking for a father- or mother-substitute can, by constant practice, readily imagine just such a convenient and comfortable god. They may call him "Jesus" and even write nice little hymns about him, but he is not the Jesus of the Gospels, who certainly would have discouraged any sentimental flying to his bosom and often told men to go out and do most difficult and arduous things.[5]

Mature believers find God as their strength and refuge in times of difficulty. But they do not take refuge and hide until the storms pass. Instead the strength and refreshment provided by God equips them to go into a world of distress, handling the storms and difficulties with the enabling power and wisdom of God.

The Bible teaches that this is a fallen world of stress, pain and difficulty. God doesn't take his people out of the world but enables them to live in the world secure and confident in the strength he gives.

Good fortune. Some people view God as the author and insurer of good fortune. Sometimes linked to a teaching called "the prosperity gospel," this view teaches that if people will do their part in faith (often taught as giving money to the person or organization teaching this idea), then God will insure the donor's financial, social and physical prosperity. Actions termed "faith acts" are considered the key to unlocking the treasures of heaven.

This view is not the biblical view of God in his entirety. There certainly are times of blessing and prosperity that God bestows on the faithful. But there are also extremely hard times and even martyrdom that awaits his devoted followers. Furthermore, none of God's people in the Bible get rich by charging other people for their faith.

The God of our group. The God of our group is most often found in churches among people who think that their group or denomination has a particular lock on God. Often these people exhibit a spirit of churchiness in a way that says, "If . . . you will jump through our particular hoop or sign on our particular dotted line, then we will introduce you to God. But if not, there's no God for you."[6] This wrong perception of God damages the believer, the local church and those on the outside looking into the church.

The believer begins to think of God as more concerned with technicalities and whether people figured out his rules than with love, justice and other ideas set out in Scripture. Of course, people outside these churches see this attitude and it understandably makes them flee from such a God.

The removed supervisor. Many hold a view of God that they might think is lofty and inspiring, but once the veneer is stripped away it is quite unbiblical. This is the idea that the God behind our vast and deep universe could not possibly be interested in the toils and troubles of 7 billion people. This is the person who comments, "God has bigger things to concern himself with than x, y and z."

Of course this does not prove that God is incapable of such care. It simply proves that our minds are not capable of such care. This person is modeling God on what we know of people. Such a view of God is way too limiting and certainly is not the biblical view of God.

Secondhand God. Many people base their view of God on what they believe is sensible about divinity (for example, what seems fair, right, good, true) in light of what they see and read. This secondhand view comes from information gleaned from others (whether recognized as such or not), rather than on what God has revealed in Scripture. This musing about God is only as good as our observations and knowledge, but it also has another more deceptive limitation. It assumes that the world and the people we are learning from have an accurate read on life and God. Of course, every reasonable person recognizes that biases, sentimentalities and faulty ideas are in all people. That makes secondhand views of God subject to the same limitations and faults.

Consider how wrong our views of God would be if we formed them by watching television and movies or by reading works of fiction. There are at least three ways that these can influence people who hold a secondhand view of God. The first stems from the writers that ignore God and religious issues. They portray life with strong characters and thrilling plot lines. We meet charming people who seem to handle any problem with grace and dignity. We also meet evil people exuding lust, greed, cruelty and more without a hint of guilt or negative repercussions. All of these people live with no reference to God, judgment or reward. This view reinforces the view that God, if there is one, is uninvolved in life.

A second way the media plays a role in imparting a secondhand view of God is by willfully misrepresenting religion, Christians and the church. The idea that every minister is corrupt and that believers are either hypocrites or saps is found regularly in books, on TV and in movies. This leads to a view that Christian faith is stupid or hypocritical at best, and devious at worst.

Third, books, film and TV can corrupt a view of God by portraying faith as centering on the outcomes of chance. Because the author gets to play the role of God in the composition, circumstances are sometimes manipulated to be mysterious, outrageous or unjust. It leaves the audience seeing life as a simple twist of fate, rather than something God has a role in.

Personal grievance. Some people find God a disappointment. Whether through unanswered prayer or suffering an undeserved disaster, the idea that God, once trusted, has let one down is the undercurrent for the "personal grievance" image of God. Phillips noticed that these people "are wanting a world in which good is rewarded and evil punished—as in a well-run kindergarten."[7] This is an inadequate view for God "in the highest degree."

Wrestling with injustice is not new or recent but is as old as ancient Scripture. The Bible has a book dedicated to the experiences of a man named Job, who lost almost all he had, both possessions and children, for no apparent reason or justice. His wife and friends said there were two possible reasons for the tragedy: either it was Job's fault (just deserts for some secret sin) or God was unjust, in which case Job was urged to curse God and die. Job rejected both.

Instead, Job lived through the injustices and did not curse God. At one point Job did challenge God. But God is God, his ways are his ways, and the role of humanity is not to second guess God. So God responded to the challenge. God's challenge to Job was effective. Job was both repentant and confessional, and the story has a blessed ending. But what if instead Job had held a grudge against God? What if he failed to grow in wisdom and faith, and instead stayed arrogant and haughty, and never got over the apparent injustices?

Who could worship or serve the God they begrudged? Those who hold grudges against God have an unbiblical view of him. What is more, in reaction to some hurt or pain that God seemed to allow if not author, many turn from God and call themselves unbelievers. Some reject the idea of God because they have a limited view of who he is.

At its core this view fails to account for the way God works. Of course, God disappoints anyone who uses him as a convenience or prop for their plans. For centuries billions of people have chosen to please themselves rather than the Designer, and this selfishness has infected the whole world. God withholds his anger and assures us that he has a plan that does not eclipse peoples' free will. Once the curtain falls, full and final justice will come. The biblical assurance is that in the midst of a world where people can choose, can corrupt God's will and can drive sinful agendas through evil means, God still manages to work out his will.

A boring killjoy. For some, God is a negative force, a killjoy who gives prohibitions rather than vitality and courage. Faith is seen as dry, lifeless and mundane. Christians are seen as stunted, pale and weak rather than colorful and full of life.

Popular anti-Christian author and scholar Bart Ehrman writes of his time experimenting with what he calls "the barren camp of fundamentalist Christianity." He spent time at a Christian college where he remembers being deprived of smoking, drinking alcoholic

beverages, going to movies, playing cards and dancing.[8] Viewing
Jesus as a killjoy is in stark contrast to the biblical God, and ab-
staining from such things can leave an impression of personal holiness that is confused with biblical holiness. The most holy human
in history is Jesus, and this was not his life. He was indicted by the
"holy folks" for hanging out with those who were far from killjoys.
Jesus drew an interesting contrast between the public perceptions
of his ministry and that of the austere John the Baptist: "John came
neither eating nor drinking, and they say, 'He has a demon.' The
Son of Man came eating and drinking, and they say, 'Look at him!
A glutton and a drunkard, a friend of tax collectors and sinners!' Yet
wisdom is justified by her deeds" (Mt 11:18-19).

Similarly, in his song "Only the Good Die Young," songwriter
Billy Joel sings to convince Virginia to leave the virtues of her
Christian faith in favor of his personal advances. Among his seduc-
tions is the line,

> They say there's a heaven for those who will wait
> Some say it's better but I say it ain't
> I'd rather laugh with the sinners than cry with the saints

Joel's explanation? The idea that a life of faith is boring and sinning
is more fun.

This view of God is simply not right. Life in God exceeds the joy
the world offers. Jesus came that we might have abundant life, not
a barren one (Jn 10:10). For Paul, life filled with God's Spirit is true
fun that the world can only imitate with drunkenness (Eph 5:18).
When Paul listed the fruit of the Spirit, joy was second on the list,
right behind love.

This does not mean that there is no tragedy, distress and difficulty
in life. Believers and nonbelievers alike face such things. But the
biblical God does not deprive his followers of the means to make it

through life's difficulties. Instead, God lets nothing go to waste, not even tragedy that seems to break someone. God rebuilds broken people, making them more suitable for his use, imbued with joy and vitality, living life to its fullest.

A fun-house mirror. Some of us see God as a magnification of our own ideas, values and emotions. God becomes a distorted mirror reflection of our self. Psychologists call it "projection" when this occurs between people, and it can also occur between people and God. This tendency must be fought on individual and societal levels. For example, a harsh and puritanical society teaches a hard and puritanical God. The laid back and lax society views God more like Santa Claus.

A view of God that is a projection of oneself may seem right, but it actually worships oneself, not God. While this may help self-esteem, it falls woefully short wherever the self falls short. It is also simply wrong. The biblical principle is that any image of God apart from God's self-revelation is an idol. We learn of God from God, not from our own sense of what God should be.

God for the elite. Humans have a tendency to classify people. When this permeates the church, it tends to produce a view that God has favorites. Some think that God has a special love for the superspiritual among us. But when we create a special class of mystic or megaholy people, we fail to see the biblical God that makes all humans brothers and sisters of equal standing. God's goal is not to produce a special class of people who contemplate mystic visions. His goal is for each person to grow joyful and fruitful as a human being.

A contract partner. Some people view God as a contractual partner, with religion as the contract. As long as people obey certain rules, God will be faithful to look after them and their interests. This makes God and life a cut-and-dried formula. If I do thus and so, then God will do this; if I do something different, then God will alter his action accordingly.

This is not the full biblical view of God. God did enter into a "covenant" (somewhat like but different than a contract) with Israel, but there is more to God than was taught in the Old Testament. The Bible reveals Jesus as God in the flesh. Jesus shows us aspects of God not as easily seen in the Old Testament. The Bible does not teach that God changed but that God was more fully revealed.

God without personality. A more modern conception of God, often deemed "enlightened," depersonalizes him by making God the "ultimate bundle of highest values." God is the virtues and the highest values raised to the nth degree. Whatever is noble and right is God.

The Bible certainly teaches that God's character is moral and ethical. He is perfect and beyond reproach. But God is more than that. He is personal. He seeks a relationship with humans. Limiting God to a set of values minimizes who he is. This may seem to hold God in the highest regard, but it eliminates the true love and honor found only in a relationship.

SUMMARY

I have used this chapter to help erase our whiteboards, so we can now fill the boards with the biblical teaching on God. This is foundational to later elements of our trial, and it also serves a more immediate purpose, as we will see in chapter four.

4

Who Is God?

(PART ONE)

HARRY FELL SIXTEEN FEET, headfirst on an asphalt parking lot. Witnesses saw him bounce off the pavement, leaving him with many broken bones, and, even more important, with a traumatic brain injury. The head injury left him confused, unable to process emotions and with memory loss. Harry was not able to attend his own trial. He was in an institution. Harry's wife, Susan, sat at the counsel table with me.

By trial, Harry and Susan had been separated for sixteen months, parting about a year after the fall, because Harry was convinced Susan was after his money. He had none, and this was just a manifestation of his brain damage, but the jury did not know that. Furthermore, the lawyer on the other side played up the idea that Sally was in court for exactly that reason: Sally wanted money. Under the law, Sally was entitled to compensation for the effect the injury had on her life and marriage.

I knew this was not Susan's motive, and my job was to let the jury get to know Susan. Once they did, they could better assess the truth.

"Your honor, I call Susan Johnson to the stand."

Susan took the oath and sat down. The examination did not last more than two hours, but the core question-and-answer sequence took less than two minutes.

Q. "Susan, what do you want from this jury? How much money are you asking for?"

A. "Mr. Lanier, I don't want the jury to give me a single penny." Turning to the jury, she added, "Ladies and gentlemen, take any money you think I am entitled to and put it into the trust fund under the judge's oversight to take care of my husband."

Q. "What? Are you serious?"

A. "Absolutely."

She then continued, with tears welling up and rolling down her cheeks, "My husband is bad off . . . real bad. He won't let me take care of him. I took a vow at our wedding—in sickness and in health, till death do us part. If my husband won't let me take care of him, then I need you [looking at jury] to help me do that. Give my money to him."

Susan was sincere, and the jury saw it. They learned who she was, and it made all the difference in the world.

As a trial lawyer, I want to examine the God of the Bible to understand and explain who he is. Many people are ready to acknowledge that there is a god, perhaps even regarding him worthy of an uppercase G. There is a problem when those people confront the world in the expansive universe. They lose track of God because he is either unknowable in such an expanse or uncaring because of our smallness.

In this chapter we examine why these views might exist and the biblical view of God in the midst of the grand universe. In that way we can better make decisions about truth and life. To do so, I call a number of witnesses.

Witness List

Alan Baddeley (1934–). *Alan Baddeley is a British psychologist and professor of psychology at the University of York. He is a world-renown expert and author on how the mind works, especially regarding memory.*

The psalmist. *The psalmist is the author of anonymous psalms in the Old Testament. A number of these have a title attributing them to David, Israel's second king—"A Psalm of David"—causing some to think David wrote the psalms. While he wrote some, the title does not indicate that, for it could also mean the psalm was dedicated to David or inspired by David.*

The heavens. *Our witness is not simply what we see when looking into space at night, but the depths of space as measured and understood by the latest astronomical science. I use* Astronomy Today *by Eric Chiasson and Steve McMillan. Both hold PhDs: Chiasson is an astrophysicist from Harvard currently teaching at Tufts University; McMillan studied astronomy at Harvard and currently teaches at Drexel University.*

St. Paul (aka Saul). *Saul was an early prosecutor (and persecutor) of Christians. He encountered the ascended Christ on the road to Damascus, and became a Christian and was renamed Paul. After a time of personal learning and growth, he spent his remaining life on the mission field, following the faith he earlier sought to destroy. Paul wrote many letters to churches that are now in the New Testament, several of which are used in this chapter.*

Albert Einstein (1879–1955). *Albert Einstein was a German-born theoretical physicist. As the preeminent physicist in history, his name has become synonymous with "genius." He received the 1921 Nobel Prize in Physics and produced history's most famous equation: $E=Mc^2$. Einstein moved to the United States with Hitler's ascendency to power in 1933. He became affiliated with Princeton University until his death.*

> **Sir John Polkinghorne (1930–).** *John Polkinghorne was a Cambridge professor of mathematical physics from 1968 to 1979, when he resigned to study for the priesthood. From 1982 to the present he has served as an Anglican priest. He was president of Queens' College, Cambridge (1988–1996) and was knighted in 1997. He is well published in physics and religion.*

NEUROSCIENCE AND THE MIND

Even among Christians, there is not always a clear understanding of who God is. Many in the Christian faith describe God with theological terms like *omnipotent* (all powerful), *omnipresent* (present everywhere) and *omniscient* (all knowing). So too some theologians write of God as both *transcendent* (beyond the limits of the universe or natural order) and *immanent* (existing throughout the universe and natural order). These great words convey deep truths that might make sense to the twenty-first-century person, but they are not always reflected in real life. They sound pious and impressive, but do our lives show that we really embrace them in a day-to-day sense?

Our minds are funny things. In *Your Memory: A User's Guide*, widely acclaimed by the *American Journal of Psychology* for its ability to instruct specialists and nonspecialists alike, Alan Baddeley explains the way our minds store memories of not only events but also ideas. Our minds associate or anchor those memories to other similar events or ideas for later retrieval.[1]

Neuroscience teaches us that we form thought patterns in our brains and tend to interpret new things in line with those thought patterns. Imagine a bowl holding one scoop of ice cream. If we were to pour some hot water over the ice cream, it would form little channels or rivulets down the ice cream. Think of those as the thought patterns and ways of thinking in our minds. When we then get new ideas or information, it is like pouring additional water on the top of the ice cream. Some of the water is naturally going to flow into the channels already formed. But some of the water will also form newer channels, or perhaps deepen the channels already there. Our brains work the same way. Our tendency is to put everything into ways of thinking that already exist in our minds. In our day-by-day walk in life we tend to view the world from the perspective of our previous existence. Yet as we grow, we form new pathways and deepen earlier channels as we come across greater experiences in life.

Let me use a personal example. In 1976 I lived on 16th Street in Lubbock, Texas (the "Hub of the Plains!"). On May 29 of that year, Saul Steinberg produced what became a famous cartoon cover for the *New Yorker* magazine titled "View of the World from 9th Avenue." Steinberg's art was a projection of how he believed a typical 9th Avenue resident regarded the world. Half of the cover picture is 9th and 10th Avenues in Manhattan. From there you see a small band representing the Hudson River. Past the river is New Jersey, although it is only one-third as big as the Hudson. Beyond New Jersey are a few names in an otherwise bland stretch of land: Texas, Las Vegas, Chicago and a few more. Past this is the Pacific Ocean (roughly the same size as the Hudson River) and three remote hills labeled "China," "Japan" and "Russia." The message is clear: In the mind of a typical New Yorker, there is little else in the world beyond New York.

As a high school boy living in Lubbock, if I had done a takeoff of Steinberg's cartoon I could have called it "View of the World from 16th Street." It might have looked like figure 4.1.

The biggest part of the world would have been my street with my house and those of my friends, and nearby Texas Tech University. Certainly, my school would have been in the drawing. Church was a big part of my life, and it too would have made it in the drawing. If I had thought about it, I would have added Houston,

76   CHRISTIANITY ON TRIAL

Washington, DC, and New York City. The Atlantic Ocean would have been somewhere, and I was mildly aware enough to throw in England, Europe and Africa. Much like a child's drawing, the

importance of each would likely be reflected by the size I made them in the drawing. Hence, Texas Tech would have been two to three times the size of Africa. The Tech football stadium would likely have exceeded England and continental Europe combined.

If you had asked me about my level of consciousness and awareness, I would likely have told you

Figure 4.1.

that I knew plenty about the world and was quite aware of things. Yet the truth was, my worldview was extremely limited. Moving from Lubbock for college changed me, and it would have changed my picture and perspective. But still, my view would have been limited, even though I would not have thought so. My map would have been fuller and different, but the map would be limited nonetheless.

The reason church would have been featured in my map is because I was living in Lubbock when I came into a direct relationship with God. In Lubbock I learned of and placed my faith in Jesus as a Savior and Redeemer. Certainly, I would have told you that my faith and knowledge needed to grow, but I am just as certain that I felt reasonably sure that I had a good grasp on who God is. God fit into my map and worldview quite easily. He was my heavenly

Father and best friend. I fit God into my neural pathways and into the forms of my mind. God made sense to me. I could understand and fathom God, even though I had an intellectual awareness that God was "more" than I knew. I thought it was "more within reason"—almost like a rounding error.

As I got older and moved around, several things happened to my view of God. In one sense my view of God expanded along with my "neighborhood," even as he still fit into my picture and my neural pathways. But over time my early views of God seemed, in some ways, childish. My world expanded so much that there was a struggle for the God of my young neural network to keep up with my personal growth and experiences. If my understanding of God did not grow with my neural network, then he was in danger of becoming a childhood God. Having known God as a child, I ran the real physical risk of him existing only in my limited neural pathways of youth.

Had my relationship with and my understanding of God not grown, as my mind expanded I would have associated God simply with what seemed to be the naive, limited ideas of youth. As the world gets larger and knowledge expands, our knowledge of God must grow as well.

This is a warning I have given my children as they've left home for college. College is a time when our thought world and understandings expand in many ways. I have warned my children that if they fail to stay plugged in, not only in a vibrant worship experience but also in a vibrant fellowship and personal devotional life with God, their own neural network will grow, but the channels that are associated with God and spiritual things will remain those of childhood, making God seem childish and unreal. That would not be an accurate view of God but a manifestation of neuroscience.

PSALM 8

One of the college experiences that expanded my neural pathways was attending a Keith Green (1953–1982) concert. Keith was a Christian singer-songwriter who died in a plane crash just a few months after I saw him in concert, underscoring the experience to me. In the concert he told of having a vivid dream of King David singing Psalm 8. Keith awoke in the middle of the dream, quietly crept to his piano and immediately played the melody into a cassette recorder so he would not forget it. He then played the song for us. The psalm made a huge impression on me in college days, and it continues to do so today. It gave a whole new perspective to the night sky, but more importantly, it expanded my understanding of who God is and why it matters.

O Lord, our Lord,
　　how majestic is your name in all the earth!
You have set your glory above the heavens.
　　Out of the mouth of babies and infants,
you have established strength because of your foes,
　　to still the enemy and the avenger.

When I look at your heavens, the work of your fingers,
　　the moon and the stars, which you have set in place,
what is man that you are mindful of him,
　　and the son of man that you care for him?

Yet you have made him a little lower than the heavenly beings
　　and crowned him with glory and honor.
You have given him dominion over the works of your hands;
　　you have put all things under his feet,
all sheep and oxen,
　　and also the beasts of the field,
the birds of the heavens, and the fish of the sea,
　　whatever passes along the paths of the seas.

O LORD, our Lord,
how majestic is your name in all the earth! (Ps 8)

I wonder whether David ever tried counting the stars. Estimates vary, but according to modern astronomy, as long as there is not significant light pollution, we can see about three thousand stars in the night sky.[2] Here is a splendid illustration of Scripture teaching about God in ways that modern science has helped illuminate. The biblical God is *huge*. Let us explore this more.

On a night of stargazing, we can readily understand the awe and wonder of the psalmist writing, "O LORD, our Lord, how majestic is your name in all the earth." Do you notice that Bible translators put the first "LORD" in small caps? That is a standard English translation for YHWH, which is the English transliteration of the Hebrew letters that represent God's own name (see Ex 3). This name was special to Jews since it came through God's special appearance to Moses in a burning bush. The psalmist, however, makes the bold statement that God's name was majestic not simply in Israel but "in all the earth." Beyond the mere letters, YHWH stood for God's reputation, for his historical actions and for his character. Much like when we speak of someone in court having a "good name," we mean his or her reputation, not simply something nice-sounding about "Charles" or "Anne." Gazing into the stars affirmed for the psalmist that God's character and reputation were majestic and great throughout the earth.

We can follow the psalmist's train of thought as he added, "You have set your glory above the heavens." While the psalmist did not understand the nature of the night sky, he knew that it was beneath God, and that God was greater than it. The heavens were simply works of God's fingers. The moon and stars were there because God wanted them there.

The psalmist then considers people. He must have realized how small he was compared to the heavens. After God placed the moon and stars and displayed all the heavens, what is a human being to him? Why would God care or pay attention to a man or a child? Yet God did, and God does. God is mindful of us. God does care for the individual. While God's glory is above the heavens, God has crowned humanity with a measure of glory and honor as well. He made us unique and special. He gave us dominion over animals, birds, fish and more. We determine much of the course of the planet.

In this way the psalmist comes full circle. The Lord's name is majestic and a cause for praise and wonder because of the heavens, but even more astonishing and praiseworthy is that the same God cares for each individual person. That the God of heaven interacts with people brings out a final resounding praise that echoes back to the psalm's beginning: "O Lord [YHWH], our Lord, how majestic is your name in all the earth!" God cares for people even more than he cares for the heavens!

Those were the psalmist's reflections three thousand years ago, and they were expanding my ideas about God in my college years. I too had gazed into the heavens at night. Looking back at my imaginary Lubbock drawing from just a few years earlier, you will notice I had not even put in the stars. Stars were not a big part of my thought system. If I had failed to grow in my understanding of God as I grew in my neural network, my understanding would have been sadly cut short.

Fast forward to today. Science has taught us much that was unknown in ancient times. We now know that most of the bodies we call "stars" are suns like ours. We also know that those suns are there even in the daytime, but are not visible because of light pollution permeating our atmosphere from our own sun's rays.

A rudimentary astronomy textbook explains that the stars the psalmist saw were a minute fraction of what is really there. Though the estimated number of stars visible to the human eye is approximately three thousand, science has demonstrated that the real number of stars in the heavens is on the order of 100 sextillion. That is 10^{23} or 100,000,000,000,000,000,000,000.

The psalmist wrote of the moon and the stars in their appointed places. We now know that from a scientific perspective the stars and moon are where they are because of gravity, electromagnetism and other forces. The universe is not a bowl placed over earth at night, it is a massive expanse of unknown size.

The sun is our nearest star, and while it appears small compared to earth, its actual size is a million times larger than earth. It only looks small because it is 93 million miles away. Our sun's system (the solar system) is part of a collection of solar systems called the Milky Way galaxy. If we were traveling at the speed of light, the Milky Way would take 100,000 years to cross. Beyond our galaxy are billions and billions more galaxies. No one knows the full size of the universe, but the observable universe is estimated to be 93 billion light years in diameter. That means traveling at the speed of light, it would take 93 billion years to cross the universe. Lest we think the speed of light is slow, we should remember it is 186,000 miles per second.

THE IMPLICATIONS

Where does this leave us in our contemplation of God and Psalm 8? Has our knowledge of God grown greater as we have grown in our knowledge of the heavens? If not, it should. Let's reconsider Psalm 8 in light of modern science. We can still embrace the opening praise, "O LORD [YHWH], our Lord, how majestic is your name in all the earth." Whether looking into space from the northern or the southern hemisphere, whether looking at incredible pictures of nebulae from the depths of space, or contemplating the vast number of stars, we can certainly understand that God's renown as Creator reaches all over the earth.

Paul recognized the testimony of the psalmist as he declared to the church in Rome, "For his invisible attributes, namely, his eternal power and divine nature, have been clearly perceived, ever since the creation of the world, in the things that have been made. So they [the Romans] are without excuse" (Rom 1:20). This passage emphasizes that people can learn of God by observing nature. What can we learn of God from the universe? Many things!

First, the heavens reflect God's orderliness and faithfulness. The heavens show precision and predictability. In other words, the heavens are reliable in what they do and how they do it. Scientists are able to calculate orbits with precision. They can send rockets that will place a person on the moon. They can speak of the future eclipses with full accuracy. Each aspect of the universe holds not only an accurate future but also a consistent past. Whether we ascribe to a view that the heavens were spoken already formed into existence, or we believe that God created the heavens with a big bang, allowing them to form by his predetermined laws of physics, the result is the same. We have heavenly bodies that reflect a logical and consistent history. The laws of physics are consistent and reliable.

The creation also evidences an otherworldly beauty. Anyone who has gazed at the pictures of nebulae deep in space has likely also thought of how tremendous it would be to observe something so beautiful firsthand. God has placed things of amazing beauty in the heavens, just as he has placed amazing beauty on earth. God's creation reflects his beauty, something that causes everyone to pause and admire it for what it is.

A final note about the way that the heavens teach us of God comes from the fine-tuning of the laws of physics. Albert Einstein is frequently quoted as saying, "The most incomprehensible thing about the world is that it is comprehensible."[3] The universe is built around laws of physics that make it possible for humanity's existence. The smallest tweak of most any law would make our existence impossible.

Theoretical physicist and Royal Society Fellow Sir John Polkinghorne likens the laws of physics to a "universe machine" where the knobs get set before the universe comes into existence. Those knobs are set with great precision for our existence. Change the rate of gravity even slightly and life is impossible. Change the *strong force* that holds protons and neutrons together and life is impossible. Tweak the *weak force* that changes one particle into another and life is impossible. Change electromagnetism's rate even slightly and matter does not hold together in such a way where there are humans.

Some might say, "Well, it's not that the universe is perfectly calibrated for human life; it's rather that life developed in this universe as it was calibrated. Had it been calibrated differently, human life would not have developed, but some other form of life would have developed." This idea is thoroughly untestable and is one Polkinghorne calls "incredibly lazy." It boils down to simply saying, "it just is."[4]

The creation around us exhibits a consistency of mathematical precision. This reflection of God shows that the entire universe bears the design stamp of suitability for humanity to exist on earth. This hearkens back to Psalm 8, where the psalmist's cosmic wonder gives way to the wonder at God's involvement with humans. In the midst of this incredible universe the psalmist asked, "What is man that you are mindful of him?"

A Word About Science and Faith

Some Christians and nonbelievers make the mistake of confusing things revealed by science with the theology set out in the Bible. Science teaches us "how," while theology teaches us "why."

Think of it like a pot of coffee. If you were to ask about the hot coffee in the pot, I could legitimately say, "The pot of hot coffee is there because water dripped through coffee beans trapped in a filter." Another equally legitimate answer could be "The pot of coffee is there because my wife, Becky, likes hot coffee in the morning." One of the answers discusses how it became a pot of coffee. The other answer discusses why. So it is with theology and science.

Science tells us how things are, while theology gives us the explanation of why things are. Historically, people have been prone to assign events to God when they did not understand the scientific reason for the event. For example, the reason the sun got dark was because God turned it out. God became responsible for the gaps in human knowledge. Assigning unknown science to God is a theological mistake. God created the world to function not as a puppet on which he pulls strings but as an entity following the rules he put in place. We can see why God uses nature and the world around us, and we can assign reason to his usage, but we should never let God be the scientific answer for murky, unknown things. That makes for a God that is not the God of the Bible. Then when science discovers answers, the "made up" God disappears from the scene.

The psalmist saw that God was not only mindful of people but also assigned us a measure of glory to rule over creation. People are not an afterthought but the purpose. Women and men are given a role, and God has involved himself with humanity, so our role can be a joint effort with the Creator.

I like the way the night sky forced the psalmist to view the world. It moves me to blow open the restraining doors of my mind. God is not what fits easily into my neural pathways. He is infinitely more than I will ever understand. I now perceive with humor the bold request Moses made of God on Mount Sinai: "Please show me your glory" (Ex 33:18). God's response makes so much more sense as we consider his greatness in light of the universe: "You cannot see my face, for man shall not see me and live" (Ex 33:20).

Of course this is true. How can anyone see God in his heavenly glory? It is impossible. For God to show himself to humanity required a miracle, something beyond the laws of physics. To use Paul's language,

> Christ Jesus:
> Who, being in very nature God,
>> did not consider equality with God something to be used
>> to his own advantage;
> rather, he made himself nothing
>> by taking the very nature of a servant,
>> being made in human likeness. (Phil 2:5-7 NIV)

Paul writes that Christ "made himself nothing," using the Greek word *kenoō*. It means "to make empty" or "to make void or of no effect." The God who could never be seen or fully understood by a human, who made a septillion stars and can fathom the movement of every atom in a universe 93 billion light years across, emptied himself to become a human. Then, once in human form, this same one humbled himself before humans, even dying a sinner's death, to redeem those God loves. This is beyond our brain cells, and it should drive us to our knees in worship, "O LORD, our Lord, how majestic is your name in all the earth!"

CONCLUSION

We all tend to see things nearby as important and tend not to look far beyond. Often, our perspective of God follows the same pattern. We think of God as near us, concerned with us, thinking about the little things in our life. To an extent, that is a good and proper thing. That perspective, however, can create a limited image of God that is not biblical. We can easily start thinking of God only in those terms. Then, when we see how massive the world is, and how the universe exceeds our imagination, we might wonder how our limited God can be the God of so much more.

It is impossible to comprehend a God who creates and sustains the massive universe. Furthermore, even if we could wrap our brains around such a God, it would be natural to wonder how he could care about each of us, small individuals on this dirt clod called Earth, which spins around a solitary sun buried in the Milky Way galaxy amidst over 170 billion other galaxies. Yet the biblical God does care. He cares immensely. He cares with a passion and devotion that is as hard to understand as his character and power. This will never fit into our neural pathways.

5

Who Is God?

(PART TWO)

I WAS GETTING READY TO TRY a case in New Jersey. I had my group of experts ready to go and was working on my cross-examination of the witnesses I expected the other side to bring to court. One of them was a scientist who held a PhD in matters related to human physiology. This opposing expert was giving a presentation in New Orleans, so I sent one of my younger lawyers to listen anonymously and take notes. My lawyer came back with a full report. The expert was evidently very self-confident, expressing everything in very absolute terms, with no room for discussion. He saw things one way, and it never occurred to him that he might be wrong. He made his opinion from cherry-picked data and was not willing to consider any further information. The idea that he was missing some important data had not even entered his mind, and at this point, his mind was closed.

This was a good thing for our side. It always seems easier to cross-examine an expert that refuses to admit that there might be more on a subject than he or she knows. Any expert who is a know-it-all defies the commonsense experience of just about everyone. No one should wear blinders and claim to hold truth by the throat; they need to consider all potentially relevant data.

Whenever I can cross-examine experts and show that they have
selected what information they will consider, excluding important
information that happens to challenge or further inform their
views, the jury rightly discounts their testimony. Our lives have
taught us otherwise. We know the importance of growing and
gathering all relevant information.

In chapter four I used biblical and modern witnesses to explain
the biblical testimony to the attributes and nature of God, looking
outward to the stars. In this chapter we continue to examine the
biblical teaching of God by looking at leptons, quarks and the personal God, using witnesses both ancient and modern.

Witness List

Sir John Polkinghorne (1930–). *In this chapter I recall John Polkinghorne to the stand. His qualifications are given in chapter four.*

Frank Close (1945–). *Frank Close is a noted particle physicist
who holds a professorship at the University of Oxford. He is the
former head of the Theoretical Physics Division at the Rutherford
Appleton Laboratory. He won the Kelvin Medal of the Institute of
Physics for "outstanding contributions to the public understanding
of physics."*

Heraclitus (c. 535–c. 475 B.C.). *Heraclitus is a well-known
early Greek philosopher from Ephesus. Our main source for Heraclitus's biography comes from Diogenes Laertius, a third-century
B.C. biographer of the great Greek philosophers. We have frag-
ments of Heraclitus's works today, along with quotes from him in
the writings of others.*

St. John the Apostle. *John was one of the original twelve
apostles chosen by Jesus. The early church reported John as the
last living apostle and the one responsible for the Gospel of John.*

IF YOU THINK YOU FULLY UNDERSTAND GOD, THEN YOU DON'T BEGIN TO UNDERSTAND GOD

We live in an exciting time. Science has opened up for us the grandeur of the biblical view of God in ways never before imagined. Sir John Polkinghorne, the Cambridge don and theoretical physicist turned clergyman used as a witness in chapter four, is a member of Britain's most prestigious group of scientists (the Royal Society). Polkinghorne has unique qualifications to say,

> There's a feeling throughout our society that religious belief is outmoded, or downright impossible, in a scientific age. I don't agree. In fact, I'd go so far as to say that if people in this so called "scientific age" knew a bit more about science than many of them actually do, they'd find it easier to share my view.[1]

Science readily explodes the myth of a limited god, but it does not discredit the God of Scripture. If we believe that science shows Christianity to be a simplistic or outmoded worldview, then we have missed the biblical testimony of who God really is.

On June 18, 2012, IBM's Sequoia was announced to be the world's fastest supercomputer made to date. The computer "is capable of calculating in one hour what otherwise would take 6.7 billion people using hand calculators 320 years to complete if they worked non-stop."[2] Now that is truly amazing. What could need that type of computing power? This computer is used to carry out calculations on the ways atoms combine and decay within the confines of nuclear weapons. The workings of atoms involve massive amounts of mathematical calculations. The numbers and sizes involved make for a mind-boggling set of numbers.

Physicist Frank Close works to break it down into everyday experiences. He explains that each time we breathe, we take in a million, billion, billion atoms of oxygen—a number so large we need to consider something smaller than a human breath for our discussion. Instead of a breath, consider the period at the end of the last sentence. That dot contains 100,000,000,000 (one hundred billion) atoms of carbon. The carbon atoms are so small that if you wanted to see one with the naked eye, you would need to stretch the dot out to the size of a football field.[3]

Scientists have figured out that as small as it is, an atom is still not the smallest particle of nature. It is not even a fundamental particle (by "fundamental" I mean an indivisible material made of nothing smaller). An atom contains a nucleus at its core, which is surrounded by one or more electrons (see fig. 5.1). To the current state of knowledge, the electron is a fundamental particle called a *lepton*. Scientists do not know if an electron breaks down into smaller parts. Not so the nucleus.

Close further explains that if we wanted to see the nucleus of an atom, we could not see it by simply extending the dot to the size of a football field. We would need to extend the dot from the North Pole through the earth to the South Pole (about 7,900 miles). We could then see that the nucleus is made of protons and neutrons.

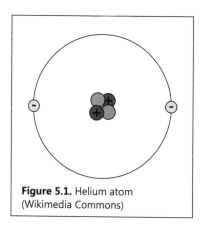

Figure 5.1. Helium atom (Wikimedia Commons)

Even these protons and neutrons, however, are not fundamental parts. They are made of *quarks*. How small are these quarks? If we wanted to see the quarks with our naked eye, then we would need to stretch the dot beyond a football field and beyond the distance between the North and South Poles. To see the quarks of a single atom, then we would need to stretch the dot from here to twenty times further than the moon.

Scientists are not even certain that the quark is a fundamental particle. Some believe quarks are made of *oscillating strings*. (There are many permutations of string theory as scientists try to establish strings as the absolute fundamental part of all that exists in nature.) Strings are a theoretical explanation of various models attempting to explain the forces and charges in subatomic particles. Current technology cannot measure or discern structures smaller than 10^{-18} meter, so no experiment demonstrates the reality of strings.

Now consider the implications of this, especially in light of chapter four. A sphere of swarming quarks, so small that you need to stretch the atoms in a period twenty times past the moon to see them, make up the protons and neutrons of an atom's nucleus. A period has 100 billion atoms, if it is paper thin. Reportedly, each cell in the human body contains about one hundred times as many atoms as there are stars in the Milky Way, which would be about 200,000,000,000,000 atoms in a cell. The human body has 100 trillion cells, so each human is made up of 200,000,000,000, 000,000,000,000,000 atoms. That means each human has more atoms on average than scientists estimate there are stars in the universe. Continue to compute that there are about 7 billion people on the planet, and we are considering 1,400,000,000,000, 000,000,000,000,000,000,000 atoms just in people. Add dogs, cats, rocks, oceans, air and everything else, and earth alone has an inconceivable number of atoms. Earth, of course is one-millionth the size of the sun, which is one of the 10^{23} stars in the universe. There is no way we can even begin to conceive the number of particles that exist. To add to the already inconceivable, the particles in an atom are just some of the many kinds of particles that scientists have discovered.

With all due respect to the Sequoia computer, it is not even worth mentioning what would be necessary to understand all the particles in the universe today. Of course, when we speak of God, we are not considering one who knows only the particles in the universe today. God grasps all the particles in the universe for all time.

THE PROBLEM

In light of what science has taught us about the nature of the universe, *how could anyone understand a God like this?* How can we fathom that there is a being so fantastic that he made and understands each particle that has ever or will ever exist? Such a being is too fantastic to understand and too amazing to describe. We have no words to explain such a being because we cannot fathom such a being. It is truly beyond anything we can grasp.

POSSIBLE SOLUTIONS

Dismiss God because he doesn't fit in our brains. We might be tempted to run from the idea and deny that there could be a God who could know such things. That approach, however, would surely be most arrogant. We accept the Sequoia supercomputer, albeit with amazement, and benefit from it daily. Most assuredly, one hundred years ago even the best scientists in the world would not have thought such a computer possible. What might be possible in another million years of the best scientific advancement? We surely have no idea. To dismiss God as possible simply because our brains cannot grasp something so large is foolhardy at best.

Reduce God to something that fits in our brains. Instead of dismissing God as an impossibility, we might be tempted to reduce God to something more manageable. Maybe God is far beyond human potential but still within human definition. In other words, we might accept that God is much greater than we are, but not on the level he would need to be to know each particle in space and time, charting each atom and exercising control over the universe. We might be tempted to make God smaller so he fits into our box of comprehension. That would be a tragic mistake. To strip God of his omnipotence, omniscience and omnipresence is to strip him of real Godness.

Make God into a super-supercomputer. A third possibility might be to make God into a Sequoia-type computer of the nth degree. God is a massive otherworldly computer that charts each atom and does the math to figure out how the universe will act and unfold. God becomes a cold machine.

Of course, all these options have a common thread. They suffer from the same error. They try to understand God from the ground up. They are human efforts to understand God in our own terms rather than understanding God as he revealed himself. God has not revealed himself as a supercomputer. God has not revealed himself as the record keeper of each electron's rotation or the billions of penetrating neutrinos (another incredible particle I have not discussed). In fact, God's injunction to the Israelites on Sinai was that they should not make any image of God. God is not easily captured by our thinking or imagination.

Look to whether and how God revealed himself. In chapter six we will consider whether it is reasonable to accept the idea that the Bible is the revelation of God. For now we note that it makes sense that we could know of God only because of revelation. This is especially true in light of what science teaches us about the structure of things. There is no way that humanity can begin to grasp the form of God, the supernature of God (by which I mean the aspect of God that is not part of the material universe), the mind of God or most anything else of substance without God choosing to reveal himself. The Bible substantiates this view and claims that God has

revealed himself in ways that enable human understanding. God
has revealed himself through relationships, stories and ultimately
through Jesus—the high point of God's revelation.

That is not to say that humans have not been able to ask questions about God and reality. One of my favorite ancient Greek
philosophers is the enigmatic Heraclitus, who lived in Ephesus
(modern Turkey) about five hundred years before Christ. His
writings influenced thinkers well past the death of Jesus (including
many in the early church). Centuries after his death he was still
regarded as "uncommonly arrogant and contemptuous," even
though he was treasured by the Athenians, read by Socrates and
others, and a copy of his writings was kept in the esteemed Temple
of Artemis at Ephesus for others to read in the centuries to come.[4]

He had an ability to see the harmony in opposites, looking for a
unity among diverse things. When writing *On the Universe*, he
noted, "Good and bad are the same."[5] Lest we think him crazy, he
had reasons for his paradoxical thinking. A splendid example is
expressed in his phrasing about the ocean: "Seawater is both very
pure and very foul; to fishes it is drinkable and healthful, to men it
is undrinkable and deadly."[6] Heraclitus was held in great esteem in
part because he was difficult to understand. His sayings were rarely
explained and left much to think through. Consider his harmo-
nizing immortality and mortality as he spoke on life and death:
"Immortal mortals, mortal immortals, one living the others' death
and dying the others' life."[7] This translation makes the passage a
bit more difficult to understand because the translator tried to reflect the beautiful symmetry of the Greek. In more colloquial language Heraclitus was saying, "Immortals are mortal because they
are living their deaths, while mortals are immortal because they are
dying their life." Still not clear? Perhaps this helps us understand
why so many in his day found him difficult to grasp.

Although scholars debate exactly how to put what remains of Heraclitus's writings into a coherent whole, there seems to be a scholarly consensus on how his writings on the universe start:

> It is wise to listen, not to me but to the Word, and to confess that all things are one. This Word, which is ever true, men prove as incapable of understanding when they hear it for the first time as before they have heard it at all. For although things happen in accordance with this Word, men seem as though they had no experience thereof.[8]

Heraclitus selected the Greek *logos*, which means "word" or "reason," as what brought meaning to the universe. This Word was the ultimate reality, and in that way he saw it as the uniting element that makes everything one. It becomes the "fundamental element" that is common and shared by all things, giving a unity even to opposites.

Many philosophers after Heraclitus seized his language and wrote of the Word as a divine force and a key to understanding the universe. Plato wrote of the Word, and according to Aristotle was taught by a follower of Heraclitus (a Heraclitean named Cratylus).[9] The Stoic school of philosophy considered Heraclitus as the source of their philosophy, and they wrote extensively on the Word. For the Stoics the Word was an impersonal force that might be better translated as "logic" or "reason." It was the supreme force that found expression in the universe's rationality.

Perhaps the most famous of the later writers to use "Word" was another who wrote from Heraclitus's home of Ephesus. One of his writings is known as the Gospel of John. The Gospel, which the early church fathers affirmed as written by the apostle John late in his life while living in Ephesus, begins by interweaving the creation language from Genesis 1 with ideas of the Word that could be read handily as an extension of Heraclitus's thought. The Gospel begins:

In the beginning was the Word, and the Word was with God, and the Word was God. He was in the beginning with God. All things were made through him, and without him was not any thing made that was made. In him was life, and the life was the light of men. The light shines in the darkness, and the darkness has not overcome it. (Jn 1:1-5)

John, like Heraclitus, writes of the Word as a principle or force that, whether men accept or understand it, drives the universe. Just as in Heraclitus all things happen through this force or Word, so in John's language, "all things were made through him, and without him was not any thing made that was made."

John's writing in the Greek gives nuanced meaning that many often miss when reading this passage in English. For example, the passage in Greek starts *en archē*, which means "in beginning." John does not add the Greek article "the" that our normal English needs to keep from sounding awkward. (This grammatical construction in Greek is called "anarthrous," meaning "without an article.") John's way of writing affirms the Word present at every beginning, not simply *the* beginning. At the origin of everything is the Word. This thought continues in the next two phrases. The Word was "with" or "toward" God, and in climax the Word "was" God. The Greek is written with great clarity and directness. The Word was not part of God or an expression of God. The Word was neither simply "divine" nor "another" god. "The Word was God."

While much of John can be read sensibly in the vein of Heraclitus and other Greek thinkers, in John 1:14 John adds a game changer to Greek thought about the Word. John makes a most profound distinction from the ambiguous and unknown Word of Heraclitus, and gives it a visible and knowable form. John proclaims the Word as *personal*: "And the Word became flesh and dwelt among us, and we have seen his glory, glory as of the only Son from the Father, full of grace and truth" (Jn 1:14).

Faced with the eternal question of the universe, John explains that divinity is not simply an idea, a reason or some impersonal force. The divine Word became human. The Word became flesh. The God of the universe, present in every beginning, the preexisting logic and reasoning, is *personal* and communicated to humanity by becoming human.

Throughout the pages of John's Gospel we read of what happened when the ultimate reality took human form, and it is what we might expect. And yet at times it is quite surprising. As one might expect, and indeed as is logical, Jesus as God had control over the elements of nature. He was not bound by the laws of physics.

Jesus and Miracles

Some think it impossible for God to alter the laws of nature, even when a compelling reason might exist. It seems to some a deception if the world does not always follow the laws of physics, even where God is concerned. Yet the logic in this claim is only there if God is diminutive in power.

God did not make a magical world where the laws of physics have no reliability. Those laws reflect God's consistency and reliability, but God as God is not himself subject to the laws of physics. God has the freedom and discretion to use the laws of physics and to alter those laws where it serves his greater purpose. Scripture teaches that those times are very rare, but we reduce God too much to suppose that he has no such power. God reigning over nature does not make the world deceptive. It makes the world reliable while also pointing to one who is even greater than the laws of nature.

Equally expected, Jesus did not simply live a magical life spoofing the laws of nature; he altered those laws only when a compelling

reason existed. Otherwise, he lived as a human, subject to those laws
as he created them. He experienced pain, anguish, hunger and other
human experiences. Surprisingly, he subjected himself to other
humans who had control in society. Jesus was never bent on establishing himself as the top of humanity's pyramid, heading a world
empire or even a religious cult. Jesus was content to teach of God
through his words and in his deeds. He finally sacrificed himself for
an ultimate purpose of God in relation to people. This is why John
explained Jesus as one revealing God through his life and death.

John described Jesus as God's Word and communication to humanity, revealing God in ways that science and vocabulary could
not. Science cannot deliver God's morality, yet in Jesus we see God's
compassion and sense of justice. Jesus rails at the unfairness of one
person against another, at the mistreatment of lower segments of
society and at the arrogance of those deluded by what appeared to
be their success or intelligence.

Jesus showed God to be interested in people and relationships.
He revealed God in relational terms. He taught about God as
"Father," even as he came as Son. Later in John, Jesus promised God
would send his Spirit as a "helper called alongside" to assist in life
(the Greek word John used was *paraklētos*). He also bore witness to
Jesus as the Rescuer or Savior, redeeming people from the ravages
of sin, both on earth and in eternity.

Another personal aspect of God revealed in Jesus is added in
John 1:14. After proclaiming that the Word became flesh, John adds
that the Word made flesh "dwelt among us." Here is another relationship word. God chose to live and exist among the people on
earth. He was a neighbor. John says that the Word "dwelt," using
the Greek *skēnoō*, which means "pitched a tent" or "lived in a tent"
among us. There is something transitory about living in a tent. It
was not a permanent residence or abode but was for a particular

time. The Word did not become a human to stay a human among us on earth. John emphasizes this point by using a verb tense in Greek called the aorist. It is a verb tense that stresses the historical placement of some occurrence. John is saying that at a particular time and place in the past, the Word became flesh, in effect pitching its tent and dwelling among us for a time.

CONCLUSION

By digging into the natural order to understand its composite parts of matter, science reveals the grandeur of God. Once we become cognizant of the seemingly infinitesimally small leptons, quarks and other subatomic particles, and once we consider how inconceivably large the numbers are in the universe, we are tempted to reduce or eliminate God altogether. We wonder how there can be a God who truly knows and discerns such vast amounts of data. If there is such a God, then what could we, as humans, ever know about him? How could we—small collections of swarming schools of quarks and electrons—relate to such a God? Heraclitus is quoted as saying, "The most beautiful of apes is ugly in comparison with the race of man; the wisest of men seems an ape in comparison to a god."[10]

The biblical answer makes sense. Common sense demands that any God who is able to comprehend and command the unthinkably large numbers of elements that exist on a subatomic scale, in such a vast and virtually unlimited universe, surely is competent and capable of caring for humanity. And we can only relate to God by his self-revelation in ways and words that humans can understand.

Word is a revelation term. It is what proceeds from one's mind and finds expression through pen or mouth. We use words to convey and communicate thoughts and reasoning. God used words as ways of communicating and revealing himself to humanity. As the Word demonstrated, God is not a supercomputer or an impersonal deity removed from the world. God the *majestic*, God the *all knowing*, God the *almighty* chose to express himself to humans in ways that humans can understand—his words and his Word, Jesus. His Word reveals God as personal, a God of relationships, of caring and devotion, of goodness and uprightness, of justice and fairness, and of power over the natural order. We fail to accept or grasp these things not because God is deficient but only because our thoughts of God are.

6

Biolinguistics and the Communicating God

BEFORE I PICK A JURY, before any trial starts, I go privately into the courtroom. I walk around and get a feel for things. Where is the counsel table? Where is the jury box? Where does the witness sit? Is there a projector I can use? If there is, is it bright enough to show videos and pictures during the brightest time of day? Is there a good-sized screen for the projector? Where is it placed? Can the jury see the witness, the screen and me at the same time?

Why do I care about these mechanics? What does this have to do with a trial? Everything. A trial is about communication. In a trial I am taking facts, opinions, ideas and more, and trying to put those into the mind and memory of the jurors. At the core of everything are the words I use, but those words also take form and expression through pictures and diagrams.

People constantly communicate; we are assimilating and filtering information almost every waking moment. Our minds think with words. This becomes important as we consider God, humanity, revelation and prayer.

Using ancient and modern witnesses, in this chapter we examine the reasonableness of believing whether a God of biblical proportions would choose to reveal himself through the written medium of Scripture. We also consider the Christian response of prayer. To do this, we need to understand how and why people communicate.

Witness List

Peter MacNeilage. *Peter MacNeilage is a professor of psychology at the University of Texas, Austin. He has written over 120 papers on the topic of complex speech action systems. He is a fellow of the American Association for the Advancement of Science, the Acoustical Society of America and the Center for Advanced Study in the Behavioral and Social Sciences.*

Thomas Henry Huxley (1825–1895). *Thomas Huxley was an English biologist famously remembered as a most ardent supporter and defender of Darwin and his theory of natural selection. He is also credited with coining the term* agnostic *as a descriptor of his own religious views.*

Salvador Luria (1912–1991). *Italian microbiologist Salvador Luria won the Nobel Prize in Physiology/Medicine in 1969. For decades he taught at MIT, holding the chair in microbiology and later at MIT's Center for Cancer Research. He was also a member of the prestigious National Academy of Sciences.*

B. F. Skinner (1904–1990). *Perhaps the twentieth century's most influential psychologist, B. F. Skinner held a PhD from Harvard University, where he subsequently taught, holding the Edgar Pierce Chair. He was well known as an author and social philosopher.*

Noam Chomsky (1928–). *Likely the twentieth century's most influential linguistics thinker, with thirty-eight honorary degrees, Noam Chomsky is professor emeritus in the Department of Linguistics and Philosophy at MIT. According to the Arts and Humanities Citation Index in 1992, Chomsky was cited as a source more often than any other living scholar from 1980 to 1992.*

Cicero (106–43 B.C.). *Cicero is the best known of the ancient Romans because of his extensive writings. He was a lawyer, a politician and a philosopher who wrote extensively, including his cited work here on the idea of divine oracles.*

St. Matthew. *One of the original twelve apostles, Matthew is credited with the First Gospel, which records Jesus' Sermon on the Mount. In Matthew's record of that sermon, he recorded the Lord's Prayer, delivered as Jesus taught his disciples to pray.*

IF WE ARE NOT HEARING FROM GOD, IT IS NOT HIS FAULT

Have you ever watched a court reporter? Most court reporters use a stenotype machine that allows them to type at least two hundred words per minute using a keyboard like that in figure 6.1. It is clearly different than a typical QWERTY keyboard. The stenotype machine has comparatively fewer letters, missing the letters C, I, J, M, N, Q, V, X and Y. It has no ability to type in lowercase letters, every stroke giving only capital forms. Unlike an ordinary keyboard, you do not type one letter at a time. Multiple letters are typed at once, each accounting for a syllabic sound.

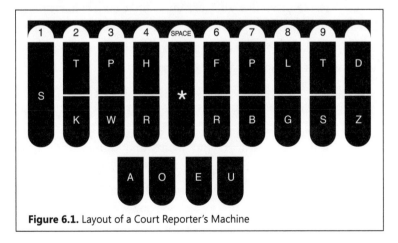

Figure 6.1. Layout of a Court Reporter's Machine

The way the machine works is based on the pronunciation of the English language. Modern English has about forty consonants and vowel sounds that work in various combinations to make the words and sounds in everyday speech. This area of study is called "phonology" and is one of four major branches of linguistic studies. On the surface it seems to be nothing of great accord. We speak, we hear, and we pronounce words generally the way most of those around us do. In actuality, speaking is an amazing feat.

Scholars believe that there are forty muscles involved in speaking. Ranging from your chest, larynx, throat, mouth and face, these muscles move as necessary to articulate each syllable, without any conscious effort by the speaker. The number of movements involved is a bit staggering. Peter MacNeilage has estimated that there are 225 muscle activations for each second of speech.[1] The rules for selecting the sounds we have in our language are not conscious; they are buried deep within our minds. For example, if I went fishing yesterday, I say, "I fished." The *d* at the end of the word that put *fish* into the past tense is pronounced by most people as a *t*. If I went climbing yesterday, I would say, "I climbed." There the past tense *d* is pronounced like a *d*. Does the brain make a conscientious decision each time one speaks these words? No. Most people make this pronunciation shift automatically, not even able to state the rule of when the *d* sounds like a *t* and when it sounds like a *d*.

As early as 1863 British biologist Thomas H. Huxley famously wrote that "The possession of speech is the grand distinctive character of man."[2] Huxley made a compelling point. Humans invent words, speak words, understand words and think with words. Marks (writing) and sounds (speech) have meanings that humans grasp immediately without consciously thinking about it. It is in this sense that the ancient Greeks used the word *logos*. *Logos* is rightly translated "word," but it also means "reason" or "rationale."

Our reasoning and thinking is done in our minds in words. Try to think of anything without your mind vocalizing the word. It rarely happens in conscious thought. It is in this sense that Nobel laureate Salvador Luria said, "Human language is the special faculty through which all conscious human activity is filtered."[3]

Beginning in the 1950s and carrying forward to today, the science of understanding how people think and process language has grown exponentially. The pronunciation exercise discussed earlier is only the tip of the iceberg in the issues involved. Three-year-old children who cannot yet add numbers readily use mathematic-like adding rules with words and sentences.

As scholars struggled to understand the acquisition of speech by humans, a number of theories emerged. In the 1950s B. F. Skinner advocated a behaviorist approach. He taught that children learned language and its rules by conditioning, being around others who used language. This view did not last long. MIT guru Noam Chomsky promulgated a very different and more readily accepted view, which is frequently labeled a "nativist" view of language acquisition. Chomsky believes that language is uniquely human and that within the human brain there is some ability to acquire and use language that is innate in a child from birth. Today, a majority of scholars seem to hold to Chomsky's opinions, in some form or another. (Still, there are notable scholars who offer other explanations for language acquisition and usage. This issue is too complicated to get full scholastic consensus at this point.)

Why is language so important to people? Is it because we think in words? Of course not. There is a core desire in most people to understand others and to be understood by others. Consider the massive proliferation of social media in this Internet age. Facebook, email, Foursquare, Twitter and many other computer and smartphone applications are the center of billions of dollars in commerce that arise from the drive of people to communicate with each other. For decades scholars have discussed the process of communication. Scholars produce models to break down the elements of communication for further understanding and study. Typical models set out two people for simplicity's sake (see fig. 6.2). One person, the *sender*, has a *message* he or she wishes to convey to another, the *receiver*. The sender determines how to put the message into words, commonly called a process of *encoding*. The encoded message is then sent to a recipient through a *medium*. The recipient receives the message through the medium and decides what it means by *decoding* it. The recipient offers *feedback*, acknowledging the received message with verbal responses, with nods of the head and even with an occasional quizzical expression. Scholars study each aspect of communication, including possible interference that can disturb the message as it is transmitted. While communication models and studies include nonverbal communication, most communication occurs through language, either in print, speech or an electronic form.

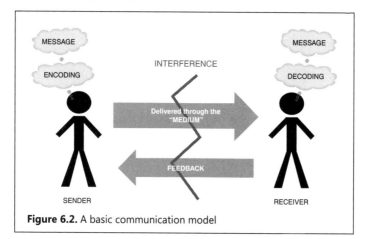

Figure 6.2. A basic communication model

In summary, words form the basis of how we think as well as how we interact with others. Accordingly, it is fair to ask questions of how language and communication figure into our understanding of and interaction with God. We can examine our own interactive communications with God, both as recipient of his messages as well as senders of our own. We are recipients when we hear from God. We offer feedback and are also senders as we pray to him.

GOD AS SENDER

Some people are amazed that today many thinking people consider the Bible to be God's Word to people—a divine revelation. To some people this view seems passé and out of date, or at least uneducated. Many academics have dissected the Bible and subjected each minute slice to a microscopic examination and then dismissed it as a nice collection of ideas, stories of fiction and loosely related realities. Many of these people are skeptical of the Bible (or any sacred text) as divine revelation. The Bible is certainly open for scrutiny. An intelligent examination of the Bible is called for, even within its own pages. I like the King James Version of 2 Timothy 2:15: "Study to shew thyself approved unto God, a workman that needeth not to be ashamed, rightly dividing the word of truth." Behind any scrutiny of the Bible, however, lies another question: Is it fair to expect that God can and would seek to communicate to people?

The case for a communicating God seems a fair, commonsense deduction. God, in the true sense of one large enough to make the stars and galaxies (chap. 3), one who is large enough to know and understand the quarks of the universe (chap. 4), certainly has the power to communicate. Can someone allege with a straight face that while humans have mastered communication, it is beyond the skill set of the deity? We dare not say that the Master of all matter struggles with English, Greek, Hebrew or any of the other estimated six thousand languages on earth. So if it is not a question of ability, why might the great God choose not to communicate with humanity?

In light of the immensity of the universe, perhaps humanity holds little interest to God. An extension of this reasoning might assert that among the seven billion people on the planet, the life of one versus another holds little interest to God. This can sound almost pious, for it magnifies God to such a degree that he thinks of many other lofty and important things besides the life of one human or another. Yet the truth is the opposite. To consider God incapable of caring about even the smallest, least noticeable person on the planet makes him small. It might not diminish him in stature ("he could if he wanted to"), but it certainly diminishes him in caring. To say that God could if he wanted to but then assume he simply has no such desire is to unfairly think of God as small in his love and attention.

This point raises an interesting contrast between the biblical religion of ancient Israel and that of its neighbors. For many pagans the gods had little desire to communicate with humans, save the rare occasion when someone had captivated a god's attention or the gods needed the services of people. In Mesopotamian legends humans were created to do the gods' work, which was tiring them out. Beyond that, people generally had to yell, shout, cavort and dance to get the attention of the gods. We see this many times in ancient literature, including the Bible. In the Old Testament, when Elijah challenged the prophets of Baal on Mount Carmel, we read about Baal's prophets crying out for hours and cutting themselves with swords and lances, "after their custom." They continued to rave on while "no one [no god] answered; no one paid attention" (1 Kings 18:26-29). Similarly in the New Testament Jesus talked about Gentiles who prayed by "heap[ing] up empty phrases" thinking "they will be heard for their many words" (Mt 6:7). Not so with the God of the Bible. He is not minding his own business but occasionally bothered enough by people to communicate. In striking contrast to all the other religions in ancient times, the God of the Bible reached out to communicate.

If we consider that God has both the power and the desire to communicate with humanity, we can then return to the communication model to see if it helps us probe the communicating God as sender.

A sender begins with a message he or she wishes to convey and then encodes the message, putting it into words or a language as needed for the medium.

ENCODING

As I type these words, I am taking the thoughts I wish to convey and choosing English words and sentences that seem to best fit my ideas. So these words and sentences carry the encoding I have chosen. I could have encoded my message using different words. In this sense I could have written the last sentence as: "Alternatively, a comparable set of linguistic sound symbols could have born out my intended ideas." I chose instead to use words that I thought more clearly conveyed my message. I also could have chosen to encode my message in Spanish, but likely "Yo debi de haber usado palabras diferentes" would not be as easily understood by everyone reading this book.

In encoding, God has many options on how he might communicate to humans. Before we even get to language, some might think God would use some awesome *big God* approach like communicating with ESP or mind control. That is not the way of humanity, however. As science continues to prove, we are at our core a verbal race. Our minds and conscious thoughts are hardwired for language. Accordingly, we might fairly expect God to use language in communicating with people. It is what people are prepared to hear and understand.

There are six thousand languages on earth today and an untold number in human history. Within all those languages there are innumerable words to be chosen to convey an idea. Those words can set out propositional truths, they can form poetic verse, or they can even tell stories. If the goal of God was to communicate with people, then we would expect his encoding to be understandable to the people who received it. This will be important when we consider the responsibility and function of the recipients in decoding the message.

MEDIUM

Once we have considered that God would choose some manner of encoding, we next consider the medium that God used. When scholars discuss media, the main ones used in history have been the oral medium and the written medium. (Over the last few decades the electronic medium has arisen, but it is so new that I am leaving it out of this discussion.) The oral medium is most common and easiest, but carries with it the frailties of message distortion as it relies on memories. The written medium has greater longevity in a reliable transmission, but it still ends up with errors in copying and assimilating messages over time.

The God of the Bible used both kinds of older media, oral and written, to communicate his messages. Repeatedly in the Bible we read of God either speaking with a "Thus saith the Lord" or commanding a prophet to record his words. As Paul spoke of the Old Testament, he called it "the oracles of God" ("the Jews were entrusted with the oracles of God" [Rom 3:2]). Paul was writing in that letter to believers in Rome who were both Jew and Gentile. The Gentile believers in Paul's day certainly were familiar with the phrase "oracles of God."

There were well-known oracles throughout the ancient world

where a person might try to seek a word or oracle of special knowledge from a god. The gods were not always willing to respond with a word; however, when the payment was enough, the god's prophet or mouthpiece usually came up with something short and ambiguous as an answer. The Roman lawyer Cicero took issue with the oracle at Delphi, citing as his example the oracle delivered to Croesus, one of Asia's richest kings, who was contemplating war with the Persians in 547 B.C. The oracle responded,

When Croesus o'er the river Halys goes,
He will a mighty kingdom overthrow.[4]

Croesus crossed the river and attacked and lost. The oracle was ambiguous. In other words, the oracle was right regardless of who won. As Cicero the lawyer challenged it, "in either event, the oracle would have been true." This was Cicero's example of why the oracles were at times wrong, at times right, and generally so obscure and equivocal that no one could understand them.[5]

Reading these messages as recorded by the Greek historian Herodotus is very different from reading the Bible. God's message in the Bible was communicated within a historical framework we enter into as we work on decoding the Bible.

DECODING

We move in the decoding process from the sender (God) to the recipients (people). The first recipients were actual hearers of the message. Even a light study of the Bible reveals that few who heard accepted the messages for what they were. Repeatedly, the prophets were rejected as false babblers. The people constantly wanted God to communicate on their own terms, not his. A familiar story from the New Testament involves Jesus raising Lazarus from the dead (Jn 11). Following this, some believed Jesus was the Messiah, but many did not. They went to the authorities to get Jesus in trouble. Consider this in light of the Gospel of Luke's recounting of a parable about a man named Lazarus and an unnamed rich man (Lk 16:19-31). This parable stands out as the only recorded parable where one of the characters is named. Interestingly, the name Jesus chose is the same name of the man Jesus raised from the dead.

In the parable the rich man has an easy life, and poor Lazarus a difficult one. Both men die, the rich man suffering torment in hades while Lazarus enjoys the bounty of heaven. The rich man cried out for father Abraham to send someone back from death to warn his brothers lest they wind up with the same fate. Abraham explained that the brothers had "Moses and the Prophets; let them hear them." The rich man admitted his brothers would not listen to them, but would surely listen if someone came back from the dead. Jesus responded, "If they do not hear Moses and the Prophets, neither will they be convinced if someone should rise from the dead" (Lk 16:31). Of course, this message echoes heavily in the Scriptures where neither the resurrection of Lazarus nor the resurrection of Jesus was heard by those already deaf to Scripture.

Part of decoding, then, is accepting who the sender is and distinguishing the sender from the medium. In other words, to adequately decode the message of God we need to see the Bible and its prophets as media God used to convey his message, rather than mere humans who themselves devised the message.

After we understand the medium as the medium, rather than confusing it with the sender, then we need to decode the medium. This means that we consider the interference that may have occurred, which in this case is often a copying error or other transmission issue. Scholars work to separate the message from such interference. Those who do this are constantly going over thousands of manuscripts to make sure they can reconstruct the best original text to be used in the decoding process. The next step is placing the historical language into a modern one. Teams of translators work for decades to make and keep translations in modern dialects to enable individuals to read and understand the words of Scripture.

Even reading and understanding a translated word, however, is not the fullest way to decode and capture the original message. Often the historical context needs some additional information to help place it into modern minds. A reference to "June Cleaver" today might mean something to the crowd old enough to have seen *Leave It to Beaver*. But for those too young to know that TV show, such a reference would be lost. Far away geography is often not understood, even where it is important in understanding one point or another. Ancient manners of writing and speaking, forms of poetry, organizing ideas and other style issues also frequently get involved in proper decoding in light of the medium used.

While many issues are difficult and require significant study, we need to remember that God wanted to get his core message across in simple, unambiguous terms. This message, in the core teaching of Scripture, is not hard for us to decode. Even among the hundreds of church denominations, a vast majority agrees with core biblical concepts termed "orthodoxy":

- God made people to be in fellowship with God. (Gen 1–2)

- Humanity sinned and drove a wedge between each person and God. (Gen 3)

- Without God overcoming our sin in some manner consistent with his character, that division between God and us would be permanent. (Rom 5:12-14)

- In a miracle God became incarnate and lived a perfect life as Jesus, Messiah. (Phil 2:5-8; Heb 4:15; 1 Pet 2:22)

- Jesus was crucified, taking on the responsibilities and sins of humanity. (Rom 3:21-26)

- After dying, Jesus was resurrected for eternity, appearing on earth as a testimony to the power of God before ascending into heaven. (1 Cor 15:3-28)

- God sends his Holy Spirit to move and teach people these truths as set out in Scripture. Without such conviction from the Spirit, these truths seem foolish. (Jn 14–16; 1 Cor 2:6-16)

- Those who place their trust and faith in Jesus' death are accorded the righteousness of Christ. (Rom 3:27-30; Eph 2:8-10)

- Jesus will come again, transforming this world and changing God's people from mortal to immortal. (1 Cor 15:50-57)

None of these concepts is difficult to glean from Scripture. They are each clearly communicated, and few who ascribe to the Bible as God's authority dispute these.

In the encoding process we need to understand the clear messages but are also obligated to deal with more difficult sections of Scripture and decode historical matters properly.

FEEDBACK

All communication models provide for feedback, which is the re-action and response of the one receiving a communication. It may be verbal or nonverbal. In fact, even ignoring a sender and the message is a kind of feedback.

The Christian faith speaks to difference kinds of feedback or responses to God and his message. Some dismiss the sender and minimize any message ("The fool says in his heart, 'There is no God'" [Ps 53:1]). Some minimize the message, thinking it quaint but hardly relevant. The Christian faith speaks to the feedback of a believer as something more.

The believer's feedback to God takes several forms. Certainly, a Christian's life reflects a response to his message. How we live indicates whether we believe it or not. The New Testament writer James pointed out that while believers cannot show one another the actual faith in our hearts, our actions most certainly show that faith or a lack thereof.

In one particular way worth noting, the believer's feedback takes a special form where he or she becomes a sender of a responsive message to God. At this point in communication theory, we have moved from one sender to two, and the speech has become a dialogue or a two-way conversation. This is the Christian teaching on prayer. Prayer is an active response to a conversation God started.

Consider, as an example, the Lord's Prayer, which is found in both Matthew 6 and Luke 11. While the words as most commonly recited are found in Matthew, the Luke passage has a prelude that places the prayer in an interesting context. The Luke passage begins with Jesus ending a time of personal prayer. One of his disciples then asked him to teach them to pray. Jesus then taught them with this prayer.

Before we consider Jesus' teaching on this matter, we should consider several points. First, the great God is not really in need of our prayers as if he does not know what we are thinking. Of course, he knows every thought and word before we form it. Psalm 139:1-4 makes this point clearly:

O LORD, you have searched me and known me!
You know when I sit down and when I rise up;
    you discern my thoughts from afar.
You search out my path and my lying down
    and are acquainted with all my ways.
Even before a word is on my tongue,
    behold, O LORD, you know it altogether.

Jesus made the same point in the prologue to his prayer recorded in Matthew 6:7-8, "When you pray, do not heap up empty phrases as the Gentiles do, for they think that they will be heard for their many words. Do not be like them, for your Father knows what you need before you ask him." Matthew uses an interesting Greek word that gets translated as "empty words." The Greek is *battalogeō*, and it refers to one who is "babbling on and on." Jesus taught that prayer is not an effort to get God's attention in order to inform him of needs that he is not aware of or might have overlooked. God knows our needs. Prayer is still important though. It is humanity's feedback. It is a responsive dialogue between two in relationship. This becomes clear as we look at the Lord's Prayer.

The prayer has six clauses, the first three clauses about God, and the last three petitions for people.

Clause 1. "Our Father in heaven." In Hebrew or Aramaic the prayer begins intimately and majestically in two words. The first word translates into English as "Our Father." It recognizes the intimacy of relationship between a faithful person and God. The second word translates into English as "in heaven." In this we see not an ordinary father but the majestic greatness of the divine Father. So the prayer begins recognizing both the grandeur of God and the relationship between the personal God and us.

Clause 2. "Hallowed be your name." With the clause "hallowed be your name" the prayer moves directly into praise. It aids us to understand that one's name at that time was more than a mere label. It stood for one's character, history and actions. Jesus taught us to praise God for who he is and what he does.

Clause 3. "Your kingdom come, your will be done." The final clause about God is one of purpose. The dialogue seeks God's will and kingdom, aligning the pray-er with God's will. These three clauses then end with the phrase "on earth as it is in heaven." The structure of this comment can apply equally to each of the earlier clauses. God's name is to be hallowed on earth as it is in heaven, his kingdom is to come on earth as it is in heaven, and his will is to be done on earth as it is in heaven. Jesus teaches his followers to pray that the eternal would break into and influence the present. It teaches his followers to take heavenly concepts of peace and work for them on earth. Similarly, health and happiness are not just future achievements but good goals for the present.

After these three clauses about God, the prayer turns to the petitions of the praying believer.

Jesus' Turn on a Hebrew Prayer

The Lord's Prayer is generally considered a "Christian prayer," and it certainly is. But it is more than that. Jesus and his immediate followers were Jewish. The Lord's Prayer is rooted in the Hebrew Kaddish. An ancient Hebrew prayer, the Kaddish dates from the diaspora Jews in Babylonia, and it closely resembles the beginning verses of Jesus' prayer. The Kaddish can be translated:

Exalted and hallowed be His great name
In the world which he created according to his will
May he let his kingdom rule in your lifetime
And in your days, and in the lifetime of the whole household of
      Israel, speedily and soon
Praise be his great name from eternity to eternity.
And to this say, Amen.

While the contents of the two prayers are very similar, the Lord's Prayer has a major distinction. The Jewish prayer praises God as a third party, but Jesus used direct discourse and dialogue. The Jewish prayer says "hallowed be his name," while Jesus says "hallowed be your *name." Jesus' prayer is a conversation in relationship, not simply a declaration to the world. Jesus' feedback response is more directed toward the Sender.*

Clause 4. "Give us this day our daily bread." In this first request,
God is recognized as the source of the most basic needs. In our
twenty-first-century mentality we might rather pray "give us this
year our yearly bread," yet Jesus teaches us to pray for our daily
needs. We are to regularly seek God in prayer. The dialogue between God and a person is not a rare thing; it should be a regular
occurrence. Paul told the church at Thessalonica to "pray without
ceasing" (1 Thess 5:17). The earliest post–New Testament record
we have of the church teaches believers to say the Lord's Prayer
three times a day.[6]

Clause 5. "Forgive us our debts, as we also have forgiven our
debtors." In this clause we recognize human shortcomings and the
inability to live as we should before a Holy God. Our lives are in his
debt, and we are to recognize that and seek his forgiveness. Part of
this reflection on the divine forgiveness should also bear influence
on the believer. We are not simply praying for our own needs, we
are seeking to change how we are toward others.

This phrase is especially important in light of this book's earlier
contrast between biblical and nonbiblical views of God. Anyone
who fails to forgive someone who has wronged him or her is wor-
shiping a nonbiblical God. One of several things is remiss. Possibly
a person fails to see the greatness of God in his supreme holiness,
which leaves the person not realizing his or her great need for forgiveness. Alternatively, one might fail to understand that God has
acted to forgive human sin. It is as if sin is too big for God's forgiveness or beyond God's care or concern. None of those options
are full and fair portrayals of the great and loving God.

Clause 6. "And lead us not into temptation, but deliver us from
evil." As the prayer comes to a close, there is a renewed recognition
of relationship, with God as leader and deliverer. We are not able
to handle temptations and evil on our own. We are to look regularly

in prayer to the Father for aid in this regard. Of course, this also assumes that we want to refrain from evil.

The Lord's Prayer is an expression of trust in a close relationship, where the role of the Holy God is not lost but reinforced. One of the remarkable things about the prayer is its brevity. The prayer is short and to the point, with only six clauses. It is not that Jesus was against lengthy prayers. We know from Luke 6:12 that he sometimes prayed through the night. His relationship with the Father was one of dialogue. Jesus was even known to repeat his prayers, as we read in Matthew 26:39-44.

INDIVIDUAL AS SENDER

When Luke recorded the Lord's Prayer, he placed it in a very important context. The Lord's Prayer (Lk 11:1-4) is followed by Jesus' parable in which someone opens his door at midnight to help a friend in need (Lk 11:5-8). In the next four verses Jesus encourages people to pray. The parable nestled between Jesus' teachings on prayer is important. The parable focuses on God's character as he receives our requests. Placing this parable in a communication model, the praying person is the sender and God is the receiver. The parable teaches us to pray confidently and expectantly. We pray with assurance, not because of our mental attitude when we pray but because there is a receiver who can and will hear our prayers.

God will respond to prayers; they do not get lost in the ether. God's answer and response may be yes, no or not yet. But we can pray with assurance that the message we encode will be received.

From the biblical perspective and from common sense, we need to be careful not to confuse God with a genie that will grant our wishes only if we ask right. The Bible calls us to pray, to be in dialogue, to be before God regularly with all aspects of our day and its needs. Our confidence comes from his promise to answer in accordance with his will and his kingdom. The goal is not to fulfill our shortsighted vision. The goal is, as set out in the Lord's Prayer, his kingdom and his will.

Paul goes even further, noting that sometimes we do not know how to encode our messages fully. Sometimes we do not have the words we need or want. Here Paul explains that God's Spirit, who knows our needs and thoughts, will himself intercede in the encoding, "with groanings too deep for words" (Rom 8:26). Our inadequacies as communicators will not stop God from understanding or reacting appropriately.

CONCLUSION

People are verbal. Our brains are hardwired to send and receive ideas through language. Our thoughts are based in language. The passage of Scripture in which God makes woman and man in his image (Gen 1) also reveals that God speaks the world into existence. If God speaks to humanity, our first task should be to listen and try to understand what God is saying. Once we are in a relationship with God, the speech is never one-way; we are called into dialogue.

This is where our hardwired brains make us unique. We are hardwired to communicate and hardwired to seek God. To greater and lesser degrees, this is seen across time and culture. Most often this was done feebly through images and shrines. But God revealed himself in verbal communication, warning people against idolatry and encouraging them to relate to him personally.

Many modern people think of Scripture as the work of a primitive people. They have no room or need for a God. They use the rules of physics and math to evaluate the likelihood of a God. If there is a God, he is so small and limited that he is unimportant. But beyond what our brains, which are truly limited, can know lies the realm of the Creator who conceived and sustains our incredible universe of time and space. Rather than recognizing something immeasurably greater than themselves, these people choose to believe that matter, life and human beings are a happy accident.

Earlier I referenced a statement by Salvador Luria: "Human language is the special faculty through which all conscious human activity is filtered."[7] Consider the importance of revelation and prayer in that light. Is it possible to understand God without hearing and reading his Word? Can we plumb the mystery of God with our limited minds alone? Similarly, how are we to process and express our praise and worship of God as well as our desire for his will in our life if we fail to use words? By praying to him, we are using, adjusting and aligning our minds to his will. We are thereby growing in relationship with God, making a conscious effort to both understand and be understood. This is a major part of daily life for a believer.

A fair assessment of the evidence should lead people to seek and communicate with the God of revelation, who has made us to enjoy a vibrant and real relationship with him.

7

Reality and the God of Truth

TOM SMITH CAME TO ME with a huge case, explaining that he had negotiated a deal with a big oil company to buy several oil fields. In spite of a written contract, the oil company reneged on the deal. I had recently won a similar case, so this seemed like a golden opportunity.

I asked Tom what evidence he had of the agreement, and he produced contracts bearing signatures. Looking closely, I could see the signatures as "Tom Smith" and the name of the oil company's vice president authorized to sign such deals. That seemed like strong evidence. I took the case.

Over the next few months, as discovery progressed in the case, the company's position became obvious: it claimed no one had ever reached an agreement with Tom. The signatures, it asserted, were forged. My next move was to retain an expert in handwriting analysis. I needed that for the jury. I also needed it for me. The more I got to know Tom, the more suspicious I became that all was not right.

Tom made grandiose claims in my office. He told me he had been a CIA black ops man in charge of assassinating at least one foreign leader. (In fairness, he cried as he told me about it, saying it bothered him "to this day.") He told me he had connections with some of the most powerful politicians of our day and offered to get me an audience with any I wished to talk to. These claims were not believable. They did not pass the smell test.

One day the final straw played out. I was set to take the deposition (sworn testimony) of the vice president who allegedly signed the contract. By accident, I had left the signed copy of the contract back in my office, and I needed it at the deposition. I was going to postpone things by an hour to get the contract, but Tom was in a hurry that day. He told me, "Don't worry, Mark. I can handle this." He then opened his briefcase to reveal several copies of unsigned contracts already filled in with the terms. With pen in hand, he forged the vice president's signature right before my eyes. Tom proudly declared, "No one can tell the difference, and we can just substitute the one from the office when no one is looking."

I withdrew from the case immediately.

Knowing what is true and knowing what is false—these are central needs for everyone, Christian or not. This is the focus in this chapter. We will examine whether it is reasonable that we can know reality or whether our entire process of knowing is flawed and misguided.

Witness List

Plato (c. 427–c. 347 B.C.). *Plato was an ancient Greek philosopher, mathematician and author. He was a student of Socrates and a teacher to Aristotle. Still studied today, both for his questions and his ideas, he is generally considered a primary voice in the development of Western civilization and thought.*

Chuang Tzu (c. 4th century B.C.). *Chuang Tzu (also spelled Zhuang Zhou or Zhuangzi) was a Chinese philosopher regarded for his skeptical outlook on life.*

René Descartes (1596–1650). *René Descartes was a French* *philosopher and mathematician who wrote extensively. He is often termed the father of modern philosophy and is quoted for his response to the search for reality, "I think, therefore, I am."*

Nick Bostrom (1973–). *Nick Bostrom is a Swedish philosopher with a PhD from the London School of Economics. He teaches at Oxford University, where he also serves as director for the Future of Humanity Institute. He has over two hundred publications and was listed by* Foreign Policy *as one of their top one hundred global thinkers.*

St. Paul. *In this chapter I recall Paul to the stand. His description is found in chapter four.*

St. John the Apostle. *In this chapter I recall John to the stand. His description is found in chapter five.*

Anselm of Canterbury (c. 1033–1109). *Anselm was a Benedictine monk and philosopher who served as the Archbishop of Canterbury. Anselm is famous as one of the first to publish on the ontological argument for God. This argument asserted that if we define God as the greatest thing conceivable, then God must exist. For if God does not exist, then the God we think of is not the greatest thing conceivable. Anselm taught that a God who was in our mind and truly existed would be greater than a God we merely thought of. So our thought of God as the greatest must mean his existence.*

Augustine (354–430). *Augustine was a church bishop and philosopher whose writings influenced the church from his day to present. He was one of the first to frame arguments around the the present effects of Adam's sin (the doctrine of "original sin"). He also framed the arguments for a "just war," justifying war when it meets certain criteria and endorsing a Christian to fight in such a war and take lives.*

In 1998, the multi-award-winning film *The Truman Show* was released. Starring Jim Carrey, the movie used both humor and satire to deliver a thought-provoking attack on reality television shows. In the process the film raised serious questions about life, truth and reality. The movie has since been the subject of many essays on why we believe what we believe, existentialism and simulated reality.

The plot revolves around a reality television show based on the life of Truman Burbank (Jim Carrey). The reality show was a worldwide phenomenon that began with Truman in his mother's womb. Truman lived his entire life unaware that he was living in a television-created environment where every person he encountered was really an actor and where the producer was orchestrating each scene for the benefit of ratings and the viewing audience. By the time Truman turned thirty, he began to have suspicions about "reality." Sometimes the suspicions were instigated by a production glitch, like when a "star" fell and turned out to be a movie spotlight. (The director tried to cover up this gaffe by having a character explain to Truman that the light at his feet was in fact a landing light from an airplane that fell off in mid-flight.)

Ultimately, to the director's frustration, Truman decided to journey beyond the limits of the bubble built by the production company. Up to that point Truman had lived his entire life in an eco-bubble constructed and maintained by the production company, with cameras hidden everywhere. Through various mechanisms, the director kept Truman from venturing outside his "world" as it existed in the bubble. As Truman tried to leave his city, the director managed to stop Truman from leaving, staging everything from traffic jams, forest fires and even a reported nuclear meltdown. Truman finally escaped by taking a small boat to the edge of the painted dome that enveloped the production bubble. The boat reached the edge of the enclosed area and punctured the wall that was painted to be the sky. Along the wall Truman found stairs and stepped out from his world that he mistook for reality his entire life and into the real world.

In the movie Truman faced ultimate questions: What is real? Were his relationships real or manufactured? Was his world real or manufactured? Was the news real or manufactured? Did his actions matter? Was love genuine? As original as the movie was, these are not questions that were invented by or unique to this movie. They are questions that extend throughout history and still thrive in certain circles today. Some might say that today there are perhaps more ways and reasons to doubt reality than ever, and the questions are certainly ones that merit discussion.

In this chapter we examine reality and truth in light of God and Christian beliefs. Some people believe they can grasp truth and reality through their minds. Others think truth and reality are too elusive to grasp at all. Most of these people are not really focusing on the Christian view of God. Many others who have some regard for God ignore divine revelation, instead opting for blind acceptance without thinking through whether such faith is reasonable. This chapter centers on what truth is and how we know truth.

WHAT IS TRUTH: HISTORICAL QUESTIONING

The Truman Show was not the first effort at questioning what is real or true. One of the most famous early Western thinkers on this subject was Plato, who is famous for his theory that what appears physically is a mere shadow of reality. Plato asserted reality was seen intellectually. His well-known illustration uses the setting of a cave. Picture a prisoner chained in a cave and facing a blank wall for his entire life. There is a fire behind the prisoner, which the prisoner cannot see, and as people pass between the fire and the prisoner he does not see the people but only a shadow cast on the wall. Never having seen anything else, the prisoner believes the shadows to be real (see fig. 7.1).[1]

I can use a table to illustrate Plato's argument. The world has millions of tables, each distinct in some way. Even as there are many different tables, there is one thing that we can all call a table. For Plato, there existed a nonphysical ideal table that is expressed in the various tables we see. For Plato, we see the physical table, but the true thing—the higher form or reality or truth—is universal "tableness," which is expressed in shadowy form in a physical table.

Plato's Theory of Forms

Plato's Theory of Forms reflects the English Translation of the Greek words *eidos* and *idea* as "Form." It is generally capitalized, in part to show the particular meaning being assigned to it. In English, we often think of form as the visible shape of an item. That is not the way Plato used the words. For Plato, Forms were not something visible, nor were they merely ideas. They were nonphysical, eternal, unchangeable, never-dying, true "Forms" that manifested in various physical entities like a shadow on the wall.

Figure 7.1. (image from Wikimedia Commons)

Among Eastern thinkers one of the most famous early questioners of reality was Chuang Tzu (who likely wrote near the same time as Plato in the fourth century B.C.). His "Butterfly Dream" is frequently cited as questioning reality. In the dream Chuang Tzu dreamed he was a butterfly with a most happy life. Upon awakening Chuang Tzu found himself a man. Chuang Tzu then asked the question "Am I a man who dreamt I was a butterfly or am I a butterfly now dreaming I am a man?"[2]

If we fast-forward to the first century A.D. we can consider the New Testament writings of John. John's Gospel uses the word *truth* over twenty-five times. (*Truth* is also used seventeen times in his short letters, 1–3 John.) One of the most famous Gospel passages is when Jesus was standing before the Roman regional authority Pontus Pilate. Pilate asked Jesus if he was claiming to be the king of the Jews. Jesus responded that his kingdom was not of this world, which must have challenged Pilate's views of the structure and form of reality. Pilate then reframed the question, removing the part about the Jews: "So you are a king?" To that question, Jesus answered: "You say that I am a king. For this purpose I was born and for this purpose I have come into the world—to bear witness to the truth. Everyone who is of the truth listens to my voice" (Jn 18:37). Jesus' claim, by inference, is that he is king of the truth. Pilate responded with his famous question, "What is truth?" (v. 38).

Moving through history, we find René Descartes, one of the more famous philosophers who wrote on the nature of truth and reality. Descartes's concerns reached beyond "What is real?" to include the question "How do we know truth to be truth?" Among his now famous writings is *Meditations on First Philosophy: In Which the Existence of God and the Immortality of the Soul are Demonstrated*, which was soon placed on the papacy's index of blasphemous books (Index Librorum Prohibitorum). This book is famous for its approach to knowledge and reality. Descartes begins the book noting the many things he had believed to be true that turned out to be false. He wanted to hold only truths that could not be doubted or proved false. Because the time involved in sorting through his beliefs was massive, he decided to go to the root of his disbeliefs. His approach was akin to chopping down a tree, knowing if the trunk was false, then all the limbs and leaves were as well. It would be quicker to fell the entire tree rather than go leaf by leaf identifying false beliefs.

Descartes's first meditation centered on how wrong he had been regarding foundational ideas of life since his childhood. He decided that the senses could be deceptive, and reminiscent of Chuang Tzu's butterfly dream he used the example that life itself could be a dream. Descartes's solution was to doubt everything, considering everything false unless he could establish it as true. In his second meditation he came to an accepted reality or truth: "I am, I exist." Descartes decided that since he had persuaded himself that everything was false, he must exist because he is doing the thinking.

Descartes then built his belief system block by block with mathematical precision to establish things that are real and true, and things that aren't. Descartes relied totally on his rational thinking to establish truth. This was quite a departure from those who wrote before him. For centuries truth was determined by acceptance of historical ideas and conceptions rather than by one's own thinking. To illustrate his concerns Descartes used a piece of wax fresh from a beehive. He wrote that all five senses informed him of the wax: it had a certain color and shape (eyes), smelled of flowers (nose), was sweet (taste), was hard and cold (touch) and made a sound when struck with the finger (hearing). Yet, when he brought the wax close to a fire, the shape changed, the smell evaporated, the taste was burned away, it melted and could not be handled without burning him, and it no longer made a noise when struck. In this example, all five senses were deceived about wax. The only way he could adequately understand the true nature of wax was by thinking about it, not by any of the five senses.

Descartes is recognized as the father of modern rationalism, or the idea that we can find the truth through reason alone. Many since Descartes have challenged this conclusion; however, his method of determining truth has taken a firm hold of many Western thinkers.

As civilization entered the twenty-first century, people continued to question reality and truth, sorting through seemingly innumerable approaches and their permutations. On a philosophical level Oxford's Nick Bostrom has made a name for himself through his writings and lectures on human potential, and for quizzing reality. In a paper published in *Philosophical Quarterly* in 2003, Bostrom argues that one possible reality is that we are all living in a computer simulation. He bases this on the idea that at some point in the future computers will be powerful enough to run simulations of what life was like in earlier human history. He also thinks that these programs will have human characters with a capacity for conscious thought. Thus he suggests that we might be living inside the computer program with computer-generated consciousness rather than biological minds.[3]

To many, Bostrom's ideas will recall *The Matrix* movie trilogy, although the Matrix idea was quite different. In the Matrix people's bodies existed in electricity-tapping wombs in which a computer was pumping a false reality into their minds. For Bostrom our entire existence might be a computer simulation.

WHAT IS TRUTH: THE DANGERS IN PLAY

For some of us the reaction might be, Why are those goofy people asking such questions and making those suggestions? Normal people know what is real. It is what and how we live and eat, and who we know, and so forth. But is it? Even on a more basic, non-goofy, daily level, it is fair to ask, What is truth? and What is real? Consider some emails we receive. One popular email is linked to a PowerPoint presentation of the remains of Goliath-type giants' bones found in Greece (or Saudi Arabia, depending on the email). This email, in various permutations, claims to be true. In actuality, it is bogus. The pictures came from a contest for computer photo manipulation. They have no basis in truth. How many other Internet legends masquerade as truth?

Even beyond the Internet and the obvious movies like *The Matrix* or *The Truman Show*, consider reality and run-of-the-mill television shows. While we know the shows themselves are not real, do we accept the ethics portrayed on the shows? Have we decided it is normal for two people to live together before marriage? Do we believe that problems arise and are solved quickly? Are these ethics true and good for us?

Beyond the fictitious worlds of movies and television, the world of marketing often presents things as simple reality with no agenda. The book *Nudge* reveals how often people manipulate others' behaviors by manipulating appearance.[4] For example, people assume the food at a buffet is laid out to comport with how people normally eat food (salad first). In truth, multiple studies have indicated that people tend to put more of the early buffet items on their plates and less of the later items. That is why buffets typically put the higher profit-margin items early in line, so we fill up our plates on those rather than the later, less-profitable items. (Have you ever seen a buffet with the prime rib station at the front of the line?)

Beyond the challenges of reality and truth in an everyday setting, I suggest that the ideas of current thought leaders also affect us, even those of us who find them senseless. Many of these are teaching and addressing the next generation. Their ideas may take a decade (or decades) to reach the common person, but they will come. The inability to locate and define truth has given rise to the disregard of science and other objective explanations of reality. For many, "reality" becomes a subjective experience. They try to define reality and truth based on what the world means to them alone.

In conclusion, there is much at play here. We have our own beliefs about reality and truth and the ethics we believe appropriate for life; we also have reasons for accepting or not accepting matters of religious faith; we recognize that others attempt to manipulate the truth and our behavior, and there are questions about the principles we use to establish truth. With these critical issues at play, how does this quest for reality fit with God?

DETERMINING REALITY AND GOD

How do we determine what is real and what is true? Living in a post-Descartes era, do we find his idea of rational processing appealing? Can we apply mathematical logic to deducing right and wrong? Or is the only option to "go with our gut" on such decisions? Should we return to a pre-Descartes era and simply rely on the authority of those who have come before us? Maybe we should avoid the question altogether and just live to get the most out of life.

One criticism of Descartes centers on his utter confidence in the mind's ability to assess possibilities and deduce the right answers. For Descartes the mind becomes the determiner of right and wrong and the ultimate foundation of truth, yet most everyone agrees that the human mind does not operate flawlessly, even in the realm of logic. For example, many who followed Descartes's rationalism did not agree with his proofs of the existence of God and the immortality of the soul. Furthermore, the human intellect will always be limited by its preconceptions, even though Descartes and others have tried to overcome them. For example, Descartes had no concept of a computer; hence, his argument that he existed because he thought falls apart before Bostrom's idea that our consciousness might be computer-generated. Another shortcoming of Descartes's rational approach concerns truths that are not knowable. For example, using his or her brain or current technology, no one has the ability to know the number of stars in the universe. As smart as we are, the limits of the human mind must be acknowledged.

These limitations of the mind are consistent with the teachings of Scripture. The mind is neither reliable as a source of all knowledge nor as the arbiter of right and wrong. Scripture teaches that our minds are wonderful creations with incredible purpose and possibilities, but they are fallen and sometimes deceptive. However, through revelation God enlightens the human mind to better understand reality, especially the spiritual aspect of reality. Further, God works on renewing the mind of the believer in an effort to better enable that believer to live by God's will. We cannot find all truth through Cartesian rationalism. Must we receive revelation to grasp aspects of truth otherwise unknowable?

Let's see what Scripture teaches about the mind, truth and understanding.

THE LIMITATIONS OF THE MIND

In the creation stories Scripture teaches that God made man and woman in his own image, which means in part that people are thinking and creative beings. Adam was able to create names for the animals (Gen 2:19), exercise dominion (Gen 1:28; 2:15), communicate and appreciate relationships (Gen 2:18-24). Adam and Eve were not all-knowing but were able to grow in knowledge (Gen 3:7-11). They were also subject to deception and able to make independent decisions, including rebellious ones (Gen 3:1-13). They did rebel and fell from a relationship of direct enlightenment from God. Subsequently they had to rely on their own limited, now-fallen minds (Gen 3:16-24).

The fallen mind of humanity was darkened by sin. Paul observes that God is apparent in the world, but people's failure to acknowledge or honor God led to futile and worthless speculations, both about God and reality. J. B. Phillips makes the point in his excellent translation of Romans 1:18-28:

> Now the holy anger of God is disclosed from Heaven against the godlessness and evil of those men who render truth dumb and inoperative by their wickedness. It is not that they do not know the truth about God; indeed he has made it quite plain to them. For since the beginning of the world the invisible attributes of God, e.g., his eternal power and divinity, have been plainly discernible through things which he has made and which are commonly seen and known, thus leaving these men without a rag of excuse. They knew all the time that there is a God, yet they refused to acknowledge him as such, or to thank him for what he is or does. Thus they became fatuous in their argumentations, and plunged their silly minds still further into the dark.
>
> Behind a facade of "wisdom" they became just fools. . . . They gave up God: and therefore God gave them up. . . .
>
> These men deliberately forfeited the truth of God and accepted a lie, paying homage and giving service to the creature instead of to the Creator, who alone is worthy to be worshipped forever and ever, amen. God therefore handed them over to disgraceful passions. . . .
>
> Moreover, since they considered themselves too high and mighty to acknowledge God, he allowed them to become the slaves of their degenerate minds, and to perform unmentionable deeds.

Humanity's failure to recognize God led to mindsets that distorted truth and right and wrong, all the while claiming to be wise and educated. Paul approached the same argument from a different angle in a letter to the church at Corinth. He focused on the inability of the base human mind to understand and accept the death and resurrection of Christ. On their own, people do not see the need for such a sacrifice or the promised eternal hope, for these do not fit into the world's logical system.

The preaching of the cross is, I know, nonsense to those who are involved in this dying world, but to us who are being saved from that death it is nothing less than the power of God.

It is written: "I will destroy the wisdom of the wise, and bring to nothing the understanding of the prudent."

For consider, what have the philosopher, the writer and the critic of this world to show for all their wisdom? Has not God made the wisdom of this world look foolish? For it was after the world in its wisdom failed to know God, that he in his wisdom chose to save all who would believe by the "simple-mindedness" of the gospel message. For the Jews ask for miraculous proofs and the Greeks an intellectual panacea, but all we preach is Christ crucified—a stumbling block to the Jews and sheer nonsense to the Gentiles, but for those who are called, whether Jews or Greeks, Christ the power of God and the wisdom of God. And this is really only natural, for God's "foolishness" is wiser than men, and his "weakness" is stronger than men. (1 Cor 1:18-25 Phillips)

For some, this seems quite sensible. For others, however, it will not. For those who find this unpersuasive, I suggest you consider the lessons of history. A simple glance at history, both the world's and one's own, bears out the scriptural teaching that the human mind is not a good determiner of truth, especially where right and wrong are concerned. Jeremiah, pointing out the sin and errors in his day, noted that the heart and mind are "deceitful above all things, and desperately sick" (Jer 17:9). Only a desperately sick mind could convince much of Germany that it was doing humankind a favor by getting rid of all people deemed insufficient or inadequate and thereby purifying the master race. The same sick mind can convince people of the right or wrong of many things. We want to believe the emails and Internet stories that feed our preconceptions and desires.

THE ROLE OF REVELATION

Scripture teaches that we cannot construct reality on our own without the aid of revelation. Paul explains that God takes an active role in revelation, and he enlightens believers' minds through the work of his Spirit. As Paul explains, God's work with people was never based on intellect. God does not reach out to those smart enough to embrace him. Rather, God reaches those humble enough to accept the truth of his promises and historical acts.

> Plainly God's purpose was that your faith should not rest upon man's cleverness but upon the power of God.
>
> We do, of course, speak "wisdom" among those who are spiritually mature, but it is not what is called wisdom by this world, nor by the powers-that-be, who soon will be only the powers that have been. The wisdom we speak of is that mysterious secret wisdom of God which he planned before the creation for our glory today. None of the powers of this world have known this wisdom—if they had they would never have crucified the Lord of glory!
>
> But as it is written: "Eye has not seen, nor ear heard, nor have entered into the heart of man the things which God has prepared for those who love him." But God has, through the Spirit, let us share his secret. . . .

It is these things that we talk about, not using the expressions of the human intellect but those which the Holy Spirit teaches us, explaining things to those who are spiritual. But the unspiritual man simply cannot accept the matters which the Spirit deals with—they just don't make sense to him, for, after all, you must be spiritual to see spiritual things. The spiritual man, on the other hand, has an insight into the meaning of everything, though his insight may baffle the man of the world. This is because the former is sharing in God's wisdom, and "Who has known the mind of the Lord that he may instruct him?" Incredible as it may sound, we who are spiritual have the very thoughts of Christ. (1 Cor 2:5-16 Phillips)

God not only takes an active role in enlightening people to the truths of his interaction in this apparently closed universe, but he also continues to turn darkened minds to perceive his hand at work and to follow his will on earth. In Romans 12 Paul says the renewing of our minds is important in discerning the will of God. A renewed mind helps us understand who we are, gives us appropriate humility, leads us to a more genuine love, helps us treat others properly and helps us overcome evil with good.

Some might argue that looking to Scripture is a denial of logic or a manifestation of circular reasoning. That is not, however, a fair criticism. If our minds are not reliable barometers, and if Scripture offers a reasonable and rational explanation that is consistent with experience, then it makes sense for us to look at those teachings.

The Bible does not render the mind irrelevant. It emphasizes the need to engage both God and Scripture with the mind. Paul encouraged Timothy to do his best to present himself to God as one "rightly handling" Scripture (2 Tim 2:15). He also directed the church at Rome to renew their minds, to be thinking right and

carefully before God as part of their response to God's calling
(Rom 12:1-2). Jesus himself jousted with Satan in the proper use
and understanding of Scripture (Mt 4:1-11). Satan misused
Scripture in tempting Jesus, while Jesus responded by rightly
using Scripture.

Because God longs to communicate with us, in Scripture we find
a resource for study, meditation and learning. We should reasonably
expect the One who does know the number of stars in the sky to
have useful insight for the small, yet incredible human mind. Furthermore, as Paul wrote, God's actions attest to the truth of his
message. His message is not one of logical persuasion, opening
truth up to those smart enough to handle divine logic and the in-
tricacies of eternity. Instead, his message is one of love and power,
things anyone can understand. The biggest obstacle to living is
death. By conquering death, God demonstrated the authority of his
message. (We will examine the accuracy of the reports on Jesus'
resurrection in chapter ten.) Here, I note the confirmation of God's
message in a powerful demonstration of events that are simply not
possible in a closed universe.

WHAT IS TRUTH?

If we accept revelation as an aid in helping the mind understand
reality, then we might ask, what does the Bible say truth is? What
is real?

The core of biblical teaching is that truth is unified and grounded
in God. Much of the Old Testament entails nuts-and-bolts thinking
about what really happened in history. *Truth* (*emet*) means "firmness"
or "stability." It is "that which can be relied on." It is closely tied
to the Hebrew word for "faith" (*emunah*), which reflects someone
or something you can rely on without being disappointed. In Old
Testament usage, truth is grounded in God.

The New Testament retains the same ideas, but John takes the idea a bit further. Like so many other areas of his Gospel, he uses terms that have strong meaning in both Hebrew and Greek circles. His use of *truth* accurately conveys something firm and stable. John was able to write in a way that brought out Greek ideas as well. John's use of the Greek word for truth (*aletheia*) represents more than half of its use in the entire New Testament. The only author coming close is Paul, who was the apostle to the Greeks.

John relates the story when Jesus interacted with Pilate on truth (see earlier in this chapter). Prior to that story, John gave several other accounts that put the Pilate story into perspective. In John 14 Jesus told his disciples that he was leaving to prepare a place for them. The disciples, however, were totally blind to what Jesus meant. Thomas asked how they could know the way Jesus was going because they did not know Jesus' destination. Jesus responded with the bold statement, "I am the way, and the truth, and the life. No one comes to the Father except through me. If you had known me, you would have known my Father also" (Jn 14:6-7).

Jesus' claim to be truth also occurred elsewhere. Earlier in Jesus' interactions with a number of Jews, he pointed out that those who truly followed him would know the truth *and* that truth would liberate them (Jn 8:31-32).

As Jesus says "I *am* the truth," he declares himself to be the one on whom people can rely. He is the measure of true reality. This calls into question anyone and anything else. If he is the truth, if he is reality, if he is the measure, then where do the rest of us fit in? Jesus turns seeking truth on its head. Truth is not found first in one's mind, one's experiences or one's logic. Truth is external to us, and we have the opportunity to make that truth part of our mind, experience and life. Truth is not found by a seeking human. Truth comes from God pursuing us.

CONCLUSION

Jesus, "full of grace and truth" (Jn 1:14), is the foundation for understanding reality and truth, including ethics, life and death. He provides the basis for understanding how we should live and what we can rely on. We are wrong if we think that we can understand truth or reality merely through our minds, history or even our gut feelings. We simply cannot comprehend God, who is the final point of truth and reality, through self-effort. Before Descartes, the Benedictine monk Anselm of Canterbury offered a more biblical approach to faith and understanding of truth. In *Proslogion* he wrote, "Nor do I seek to understand that I may believe, but I believe that I may understand. For this, too, I believe, that, unless I first believe, I shall not understand." Anselm was not against using one's mind, even to come to belief in God, but he saw the understanding that came from revelation as a catalyst for insight and thinking. This was similar to Augustine's comment in a sermon on John 7:14-18, where he said: "Therefore do not seek to understand in order to believe, but believe that you might understand."[5]

We know truth through using our minds in conjunction with revelation. We rely on revelation, even as we understand and interpret it with our minds, knowing that God is at work renewing our minds. This becomes not only our way of knowing but also the truth we seek to know. For some, it becomes an "aha" moment—the point when they recognize, "Yes, this makes sense."

This raises ultimate questions: Does life at its core make sense? Are we anything special? Are we merely a computer program or a dream? Are we living in a real world where things are knowable and have meaning? Does our behavior make a difference?

We have options on how to approach these questions, but the answers are defined by how we come to them. If we build from ourselves alone, we will come to a dead end. Yet we fight such conclusions. We intuitively know that the world is real and there is meaning. We think, *The ideas of people like Nick Bostrom are interesting, but no one* really *believes that stuff!*

Weighing all of the options, the biblical answer is much more sensible and aligned with what we see, feel and experience. It makes sense of the nitty-gritty concerns of day-to-day life. When we deal with a coworker, friend or classmate, we are with a real person who has real problems. Each encounter is an opportunity to make a difference. There is something beyond us that defines reality and puts it into perspective. This truth changes who we are because it draws us into a relationship with the real God who seeks us out in love and caring.

8

Right, Wrong and the Moral God

SO MANY CASES ULTIMATELY hinge on a simple value decision: what is right and what is wrong.

I was picking the jury in a case in a small town in Texas. Among the fifty prospective jurors sat the pastor from the largest church in town. We had limited information about each potential juror, and included on his form under the line asking about employment was the single word—"Pastor."

Early on, my questions were directed to the pastor. I asked him, "Pastor, have you been called to jury duty before?"

"Many times," he answered.

"How often have you made the jury?" I probed.

"Never!" he replied with a chuckle as he crossed his arms. My next question was, "Do you know why?"

He said, "I have my suspicions."

I explained that lawyers are afraid to put preachers on the jury because successful preachers are leaders. Lawyers fear leaders on the jury unless they know which direction the leader will lead. The preacher nodded, as did many other prospective jurors.

My next chore was obvious. I had to decide which way the preacher would lead in the case. I asked him, "Do you believe in right and wrong?"

"Yes, of course," he replied.

"What about lying? Is it right or wrong?"

"Wrong," he told me.

I pushed further, "Even if you're lying to get out of trouble?"

"Yup," he answered.

I then looked out to the panel and proclaimed, "I won't be the lawyer striking you from this jury!"

I wanted the jury to know that if the pastor did not make the panel, it would be because the other side was afraid of the truth. My case was built on proving the other side was lying to escape responsibility.

The pastor did make the jury, and the case played out along the lines anticipated. It was a case rooted in honesty versus deception— right and wrong.

Having now examined the kind of God that must exist in accordance with the universe and Scripture, and considering the reasonableness of his communicating with humanity, and the truth that is understood through that communication, I now approach the issue of morality. Many people sense the rhythm of right and wrong; it is something they "feel in their gut." But when asked to explain or examine the basis for their beliefs, they fall short of any logical explanation. I place these issues into examination in this chapter.

Witness List

Otto Ohlendorf (1907–1951). *Otto Ohlendorf was a convicted Nazi war criminal put on trial in Nuremberg after World War II. Following his conviction, he was executed.*

Hermann Graebe (1900–1986). *Hermann Graebe was a German engineer who witnessed mass murdering of Jews and testified to what he saw in the Nuremberg trials.*

Matthew White. *The* New York Times *has called Matthew White, from Richmond, Virginia, a "numbers freak." He prefers to call himself an "atrocitologist" for his work on the statistics of atrocities. He is best known for his book used here,* The Great Big Book of Horrible Things.

Charles Darwin (1809–1882). *Charles Darwin was an English naturalist made famous for his book* On the Origin of the Species, *which set out the theory of natural selection as a basis for the evolution of life.*

Herbert Spencer (1820–1903). *Herbert Spencer was an English evolutionist made famous for his phrase "survival of the fittest."*

Friedrich Wilhelm Nietzsche (1844–1900). *Friedrich Nietzsche was a German scholastic who wrote in many areas including philosophy. He is notable for his writings on the death of God and the rise of the superman ("Übermensch").*

Adolf Hitler (1889–1945). *Needing no real introduction, Adolf Hitler was the German chancellor from 1933–1945. His actions led to World War II and the atrocities perpetrated by Nazi Germany on millions of Jews and other outcast people.*

Euthyphro (5th century B.C.). *Euthyphro was a young man whose conversation with the Greek philosopher Socrates was written by Plato. The conversation centered on how people know what is right or wrong.*

Clive Staples (C. S.) Lewis (1898–1963). *An academician at Oxford and Cambridge, C. S. Lewis is famous for his writings on many aspects of Christian faith as well as his fictional writings and poetry.*

On September 15, 1935, Germany passed the Nuremberg Laws that stripped Jews of citizenship and gave them status as "subjects." Jews were not allowed to marry non-Jews, and over the course of the next few years, being Jewish itself was basically made illegal. Jews couldn't serve in public office or work as journalists, broadcasters, farmers, teachers or actors. They were not allowed to work in the financial sector or as lawyers or doctors. In many towns they were not even allowed entrance. In others they were not allowed to buy groceries, drugs or medicines.[1] Of course, these laws were Hitler's warmup. The ultimate atrocities occurred later both in the villages and concentration camps where Jews were used for human experimentation, forced to live in the most inhumane conditions and frequently worked to death or subjected to mass murder. Hitler and Nazi Germany went about a methodical genocide that was internally termed the "final solution" to what Hitler termed "the Jewish problem."

After the war the trials of Nazi war criminals were held in Nuremberg, the same city that birthed the anti-Jewish laws. Reading the transcripts of the trials readily shows the callous attitudes of many leading Nazis who detailed their crimes in a cavalier tone. Thirty-eight-year-old head of the Central Security Office, Otto Ohlendorf, detailed how matter-of-factly the Nazis often went about it:

> The Einstatz [a "Special Action Group" in charge of exterminating Jews] unit would enter a village or town and order the prominent Jewish citizens to call together all Jews for the purpose of "resettlement." They were requested to hand over their valuables and shortly before execution to surrender their outer clothing. They were transported to the place of executions, usually an antitank ditch, in trucks—always only as many as could be executed immediately. In this way it was attempted to keep the span of time from the moment in which the victims knew what was about to happen to them until the time of their actual execution as short as possible.
>
> Then they were shot, kneeling or standing, by firing squads in a military manner and the corpses were thrown into the ditch.[2]

More graphic details were given by German engineer Hermann
Graebe, who testified to Einstatz executions at Dubno in the Ukraine:

The people who had got off the trucks—men, women and
children of all ages—had to undress upon the order of an S.S.
man, who carried a riding or dog whip. They had to put down
their clothes in fixed places, sorted according to shoes, top
clothing and underclothing. I saw a heap of shoes of about
800 to 1,000 pairs. . . .

Without screaming or weeping these people undressed,
stood around in family groups, kissed each other, said fare-
wells and waited for a sign from another S.S. man, who stood
near the pit. . . .

An old woman with snow-white hair was holding a one-
year-old child in her arms and singing to it and tickling it. The
child was cooing with delight. The parents were looking on
with tears in their eyes. The father was holding the hand of a
boy about 10 years old and speaking to him softly; the boy
was fighting his tears. The father pointed to the sky, stroked
his head and seemed to explain something to him.

At that moment, the S.S. man at the pit shouted something to his comrade. The latter counted off about twenty
persons and instructed them to go behind the earth mound.
. . . I remember a girl, slim and with black hair, who, as she
passed close to me, pointed to herself and said: "twenty-
three years old."

I walked around the mound and found myself confronted
by a tremendous grave. People were closely wedged together
and lying on top of each other so that only their heads were
visible. . . . Some of the people were still moving. . . . I looked
for the man who did the shooting. He was an S.S. man, who
sat at the edge of the narrow end of the pit, his feet dangling

into the pit. He had a tommy gun on his knees and was smoking a cigarette.[3]

While we would love to write off these actions as a singular tragedy of human history, the truth is, similar horrific actions have occurred much too often. Noted historical statistician Matthew White gives the consensus opinion that the mass brutality of Southwest Africa (the Congo) in the early twentieth-century killed 10 million people, cutting the population in half. In Cambodia's ethnic cleansing of the late 1970s, about 21 percent of the population was killed. While accumulating the best data he can, the well-published White asks, Who was the bloodiest tyrant of the twentieth century? His educated response? We don't know![4]

One of the saddest facts of the twentieth century is that scholars cannot decide between Adolf Hitler, Mao Zedong or Joseph Stalin as the person responsible for the most deaths. More people died under Mao (40 million), but it is difficult to determine how many were deliberate deaths and how many were passive deaths from the economic restructuring and famines. For more "deliberate killings," Hitler rises to the top with 34 million, but his numbers include military deaths in battle. If only cold-blooded murder of unarmed noncombatants is counted, Stalin leads with 20 million.

The United States State Department analyzed the Serbian forces' ethnic cleansing of Kosovar Albanians in Kosovo between March and late June of 1999. Ninety percent of the Kosovar Albanian people were forcibly expelled from their homes, and about 10,000 were summarily executed in mass killings in less than four months. The accounts of forcible rape and other atrocities are well known, even though they were clearly underreported.[5]

In examining this recent history I want to probe several questions about morality. As space dictates limitations on our discussion, I ask these questions with Hitler and Germany as our focus: (1) Can we uncover any reason why Hitler and others would do such a thing? (2) Can we affirm that what Hitler did was morally wrong? If so, how do we know it was wrong?

These questions can be asked about any number of wrongs, but I have purposely chosen actions so heinous that most people readily concede they were immoral, so much so that it does not even bear examination. Most would readily say, "Of course Hitler was wrong! Every normal person knows that, and it is pointless to waste time and energy explaining why!" Notwithstanding such a protest, we will examine these questions anyway, in hopes of pointing out that for many, the examination of morality evidences a belief in a biblical God.

WHY DID HITLER ATTEMPT JEWISH GENOCIDE?

I will begin this section by setting out certain limitations. We have no interview of Hitler after the fact. We have no notes of his weekly visits to a psychologist, where he explained his actions with candor and forthrightness. I also write this comment neither as an analyst with particular skill nor as a historian, but rather as a trial lawyer. The question I can readily answer is what defense would I assert in a courtroom if called on to defend Hitler. In that scenario I would argue that Hitler and many of his henchmen could have acted as they did, thinking they were acting appropriately.

To better understand some of this, we need to put ourselves into a more historical frame of mind, leaving behind our own experiences and values, and trying to submerge ourselves in that of others. In 1859 Charles Darwin rocked the world with his publication *On the Origin of Species*. Darwin introduced the world to the theory that "natural selection" produced an evolution of life and species. Natural selection was premised on the idea that while species reproduce, food supplies stay relatively constant. The limited availability of food instills a struggle for survival among the growing numbers of offspring. Therefore individuals more suited to the environment survive and thrive, while those less suited to the environment do not.

We can see Darwin's idea in the full title of his work: *On the Origin of Species by Means of Natural Selection, or the Preservation of Favoured Races in the Struggle for Life* (see fig. 8.1).

British philosopher and biologist Herbert Spencer was a prolific writer on evolution, both before and after Darwin.

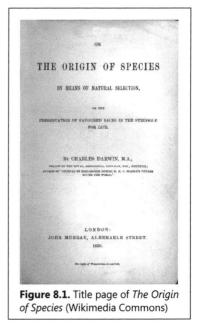

Figure 8.1. Title page of *The Origin of Species* (Wikimedia Commons)

Spencer is credited with first coining the phrase "survival of the fittest" in his *Principles of Biology* published in 1864 (see fig. 8.2). From a biological perspective this phrase referenced being fit for a particular environment; however, it was extended beyond the realm of biology. It became a moniker for the idea that the better races would thrive, while those less fit would not. This was readily applied to economics and other social areas. The idea took fuller form as many began to advocate that progress for hu-

Figure 8.2. Herbert Spencer (Wikimedia Commons)

manity was rooted in this principle. Let the better people reproduce and continue to evolve, while those less fit die out.

Into the German intellectual world at this time came Friedrich Wilhelm Nietzsche, the son of a Lutheran pastor and a marvelously clever writer and fairly original thinker (see fig. 8.3). Nietzsche began his studies in theology as well as philology (the study of language). But by the age of twenty he had abandoned faith in God, believing that historical research had trashed any truth behind Jesus and the Gospel stories. Nietzsche was well aware of Darwin's works as well as others he read in areas of philosophy and science.

Figure 8.3. Friedrich Wilhelm Nietzsche (Wikimedia Commons)

Nietzsche wrote on a number of subjects. One of his later works was titled *Beyond Good and Evil: Prelude to a Philosophy of the Future*, first published in 1886. The work thrashed most conventions of his day and included derogatory statements about philosophers: "For they act as if they had discovered and acquired what are actually their opinions . . . basically, however, they are using reasons sought after the fact to defend a pre-existing tenet."[6] In other words, philosophers do not logically reach conclusions; they have the conclusion and then try to use logic to justify what they want to believe. This idea will come in usefully later in this chapter.

Nietzsche's main concern in his argument centered on the philosophers' approach to determining what is good and evil. Nietzsche was appalled that most thought there was an absolute or objective right and wrong. Repeatedly, Nietzsche indicted those who hold some moral view (he termed it a "moral prejudice") and masquerade such as "truth." Nietzsche believed that deep in history, in what he termed the "PRE-MORAL period of mankind," the value of an action, whether it was "good or bad," was inferred from its consequences. Nietzsche then indicted the period of history when good or bad was judged by the origin of the action (i.e., what were the actor's intentions?) rather than the result.

Hand in hand with Nietzsche's challenge to moral absolutes came his views about the future of the human race. Nietzsche famously wrote of the arrival of an Übermensch, typically translated a "Superman" or "Above-Human," in his 1883 work, *Thus Spoke Zarathustra*. This work covered the teachings and travels of a fictional character named Zarathustra. In the work, Zarathustra announced, "God has died," which is deemed a good thing! God was humanity's "greatest danger," holding humankind back from progressing into "Superhumans" or "Overhumans."

The true hope for humanity was to come from a future "Superman." In this proclamation Nietzsche, through his character Zarathustra, charted the evolution of humanity from worm through ape to man. For humankind today, the ape heritage is proclaimed a painful embarrassment. In like manner, Nietzsche/Zarathustra taught, the human of today will be an embarrassment to the future Superman. Humanity, according to Nietzsche/Zarathustra, was the middle evolutionary state between apes and the Superhumans.

How is man to get to this higher evolved state? "The human being must become better and more evil." Nietzsche turned much thinking on its head, reclaiming evil as good. Nietzsche's character Zarathustra explained, "For evil is the human's best strength. 'The human being must become better and more evil'—thus I teach. What is most evil is necessary for the Overhuman's best."[7]

Hitler was eleven years old when Nietzsche died. At the end of 1924 Hitler was released from serving a year in prison, where he dictated much of his first volume, eventually titled *Mein Kampf* (meaning "My Struggle," an echo of the German translation of Darwin's book's mantra "the struggle for survival"). The book was a combination of autobiography, political manifesto and propaganda. The book sets out his promise of a grand future for Germany and for humanity. Hitler laid the difficulties of Germany's past at the doorstep of Jews and Marxists. He moved his people toward "racial hygiene," working to eliminate not only Jews but also the disabled, those with serious mental or physical handicaps, homosexuals, Poles and other "undesirable people."[8]

In short, Hitler worked to produce the master race, the next evolutionary step in the journey from worm to Superhuman. Hitler's actions were consistent with those who interpreted Social Darwinism as a notion that the races were unequal and some were more biologically fit to evolve than others. It also fit Nietzsche's idea that humanity was set to evolve to something greater and that evil was not absolute, but rather something to be judged by its consequences. Achieving the greater person through means some might deem "evil" was actually the higher and better good for the course of humanity. Though Nietzsche was gone by the time Hitler rose to power, Nietzsche's sister, Elisabeth Förster-Nietzsche (1846–1935), continued to edit and publish Nietzsche's works, being his chief promoter even in his death. Elisabeth set up the "Nietzsche Archives," which Hitler visited on multiple occasions and the Nazi government supported financially and otherwise (see fig. 8.4). Elisabeth corresponded with Hitler, and Hitler attended her funeral.

Examining some of the bases that might have informed Hitler's positions, we will now move to the more important questions of the morality of these actions and why they were evil. These questions continue to appear in the post-Hitler age of human trafficking, sexual abuse, torture and murder.

Figure 8.4. Hitler visiting Nietzsche's sister at the Nietzsche Archive, October 1935 (Art Resources)

THE IMMORALITY OF HITLER

Most everyone readily affirms that Hitler's actions were evil. I want to hone in on why we can be so certain his actions were immoral. It is not enough simply to state "I just know it was wrong." There must be some reasoning offered or else right and wrong are merely the feelings of the person being asked. One says "I think it is wrong," while another says the opposite. In the world of suggestions, the ideas fall into certain distinct camps:

1. *Right and wrong is decided by what works to assist society.* Of course, Nietzsche and others believed that right and wrong is decided by what works to assist society, which could readily be used to support Hitler's actions and agenda. We might quibble over the merits of what it means to "assist" society, but if people believe that accelerating human evolution is good, then it leaves them in a position that could justify the Nazi horrors.

2. *Right and wrong is decided by what works to assist an individual.* Closely aligned to the first suggestion is the belief that right and wrong is decided by what works to assist an individual. But here the issue is defined by what serves an individual rather than society as a whole. Of course, this is similarly inadequate for explaining why Hitler's actions were evil. It seemed to assist Hitler as well as his agenda to further the future of evolution to a Superhuman. A related idea is that how one feels determines right and wrong. This removes the language of right and wrong from objective meaning and does not allow us to say that Hitler's actions were wrong but rather that they were wrong to us. If this view of right and wrong is correct, then a person or group with power and insight could condition society to accept certain morals, and we could walk right back into a Third Reich. Propaganda, films, speeches, social pressure, the lure of power and more become the tools of the chosen few to mold right and wrong into whatever serves their purposes, and people blithely buy it, simply "sensing" his or her morality.

3. *Right and wrong is decided by whatever certain people think.* A democratic approach to morality with several permutations is the belief that right and wrong is decided by whatever certain people think. Right and wrong can be what 51 percent or more (two-thirds? three-fourth?) of people approve or think. One might also argue that the people who decide right and wrong should only be a segment of society, for example, the intelligentsia or maybe the more mature (over 18? over 21?). Some might even argue that a smaller, elite group of individuals should decide right and wrong. In all its permutations this source of values falls woefully short in proving Hitler evil. After all, the electorate in Germany duly appointed him Chancellor, heading a coalition government in the German Reichstag (par-

liament). From there, his final rise to absolute power was done within the legislative process, in a sense then being approved by the government of the people.

4. *Right and wrong is not decided; it simply exists as a truth, much like mathematics does.* Another approach is that right and wrong are part of the universe's truths. Much like two plus two equals four, certain things are just "wrong." There is no real listing of these moral truths; they are uncovered just as mathematical truths are uncovered. Over time we learn of these ethical truths through experience in society and life. There is something about this view that is alluring. It asserts an *absolute* right and wrong that is objective, even as it steers clear of an argument for or against the existence of God. Among the difficulties with this view is its inability to justify any given truth against another without appealing to what one "just seems to know." This is precisely Nietzsche's complaint against philosophers:

> They all pose as though their real opinions had been discovered and attained through [logic] . . . whereas, in fact, a prejudiced proposition, idea, or "suggestion," which is generally their heart's desire abstracted and refined, is defended by them with arguments sought out after the event.[9]

5. *Right and wrong is whatever God has commanded.* The belief that right and wrong is whatever God has commanded might seem quite simple, especially in a book on God, but it is not necessarily so. Most discussions of right and wrong among philosophers eventually get around to a dialogue between Socrates and Euthyphro, written by Plato hundreds of years before Christ. As an old man Socrates was headed to court to face indictment for ruining the young men of Athens. On the way, he met Euthyphro, a young man who was headed to court trying

to ruin an old man (his father). The two began discussing good and evil, and Socrates pushed Euthyphro into answering the question "What is good?" Euthyphro's answer eventually became "what all the gods love is holy" while "what they all hate is unholy." Socrates then asked the pointed question whether something is holy because the gods love it or whether the gods love it because it is holy. This is frequently called "Euthyphro's dilemma."

Does God command acts that are morally good because they are morally good, or do the acts achieve the status of "morally good" because God commands them? If I take this idea out of the abstract and plug in something more concrete, then it might help us understand the distinction. Consider the Ten Commandments. Did God command the Ten because they are good, or do the Ten Commandments become good because God commanded them?

If we assume the first position is true, namely, that there are independent moral standards (the "good") that God has then commanded, then we are saying God is bound by something outside of himself. God becomes "good" because God measures up to this moral standard. C. S. Lewis saw this as voiding *good* of any real meaning:

> To say that the moral law is God's law is no final solution. Are these things right because God commands them or does God command them because they are right? If the first, if good is to be defined as what God commands, then the goodness of God Himself is emptied of meaning and the commands of an omnipotent fiend would have the same claim on us as those of the "righteous Lord."[10]

If we assume the second position is true, and "good" is good because God commands it, then God is no longer a lawgiver, he is simply a means of transmission. God is a law revealer.

Euthyphro and Socrates came to their discussion with preconceived notions that presented a dilemma on God and morality. The Greeks had notoriously limited gods. In fact, earlier in their dialogue Euthyphro answered what was right and wrong by simply pointing to the gods and what they hold dear and holy. Socrates then pointed out that the gods often differed, one favoring something that was despised by another. This moved Euthyphro to modify his explanation of morality to what was good and dear to all the gods—in other words, the things to which all the gods could agree. This gives us a clue to the inherent problem of Euthyphro's dilemma, which is simply explained: Euthyphro's gods were all too inadequate.

THE MORALITY OF GOD

If Socrates asked Euthyphro the question posed in Plato's dialogue in a twenty-first-century American courtroom, the opposing lawyer might well stand up and object, claiming, "Socrates assumes facts not in evidence." (The objection could also be called "begging the question.") The objection is based on the idea that there are only two choices offered and Euthyphro is stuck with choosing from the two. Either (A) God is good because he commanded good deeds, or (B) deeds are good because God commanded them. Euthyphro's dilemma is based on either A or B, as if the only choices are A or B; the dilemma asks, is it A or B? Yet there is at least one other possibility beyond A and B. It could also be C. The biblical view of God goes beyond A and B. Euthyphro's dilemma does not fit well with the biblical God.[11]

Before stating the third option outright, let's consider some biblical passages that lead us to it. The passages we will consider revolve around two different words: *law* and *righteousness* (also known as "good").

Law in the Bible. The word *law* appears in hundreds of verses in both the Old and New Testaments. The word can convey different meanings in different contexts. Sometimes, *law* refers to the many commands God delivered to Moses on Mount Sinai. These numerous examples include God calling various rituals "laws" (e.g., Lev 6:9, 14, 25; 7:1). Sometimes the word *law* refers specifically to the Ten Commandments, as when God commanded Moses to come up on the mountain and wait "that I may give you the tablets of stone, with the law and the commandment, which I have written for their instruction" (Ex 24:12). Sometimes the reference is not to the law of Moses. Hundreds of years before Moses, God commented on Abraham keeping God's commandments, statutes and laws (Gen 26:5). At times, *law* refers to the rules of society and the statutes that people lived under (2 Chron 19:10; Ezra 7:24, 26).

Not only does *law* have different meanings in the Bible, but it also had different functions in society. There seem to be at least three functions of the law in the Bible.

1. The law functioned as a check on the behavior of the unholy. In this sense Paul wrote of the "law" as something "not laid down for the just but for the lawless and disobedient, for the ungodly and sinners, for the unholy and profane, for those who strike their fathers and mothers" (1 Tim 1:9-11).

2. It was also an instruction guide for the godly, teaching right and holy behavior.

3. The law also pointed to the crucified Christ as a necessary solution to human errors. Paul made this point in his letter to the church at Galatia, explaining, "Now before faith came, we were held captive under the law, imprisoned until the coming faith would be revealed. So then, the law was our guardian until Christ came, in order that we might be justified by faith" (Gal 3:23-24).

The different definitions of and roles of the law stem from a common point. Each finds its roots in the character and nature of God. The character and nature of God is to express holy and right behavior. Certainly, the failure of humans to measure up to God's character and nature points to a need for some intervention to deal with our inadequacies. This is necessitated by God's goodness and righteousness.

"Righteousness" and "goodness" in the Bible. Three centuries before Socrates the Old Testament prophet Amos was setting out ideas of righteousness and goodness and their relationship to God. Secular scholars generally recognize these writings as novel in the world at the time. Norman Snaith included the prophet Amos with several of his contemporary prophets when he wrote, "Their message is recognized by all as making a considerable advance on all previous ideas."[12] For Amos and the prophets, goodness and righteousness were wrapped up in a Hebrew word *tzedek*. The essence of the Hebrew *tzedek* is not some abstract idea of good but an action or activity that we would call good. In Hebrew thought goodness is not simply an idea; it is an expression of right behavior that establishes God's will in the land. Goodness is the norm that depends entirely on the nature of God.

We see this expressed in the theology of both Jesus and Paul. In Matthew 19:16-22 a rich young man asks Jesus what "good" deed he should do to have eternal life. Jesus responds, "Why do you ask me about what is good? There is only one who is good. If you would enter life, keep the commandments." Paul echoes this same idea in his letter to the Roman Christians when he writes that "none is righteous. . . . No one does good, not even one" (Rom 3:10-12). Both of these accounts illustrate an idea of good that is intimately tied to the usages of law.

This brings us to the biblical idea of goodness that distinguishes

Euthyphro's dilemma. Revealed Scripture teaches that God is a moral being. By that I mean God is not some robot programmed to do good consistently. God actually has morality inherent in his essence. God has a moral nature. If we were to examine God's actions and behaviors, then we could give them the label "good." That is not because God's behaviors meet our standard of goodness. It is because we derive our concept of good from his nature.

Let's consider an example to help illustrate this point. Consider a rare child that is born with a kind nature. From the earliest age this child reacts to events with kindness and gentleness. Now, let's ask Euthyphro's questions about the child: "Are these behaviors kind because they are coming from a kind child? Or is this child kind because the child is doing kind behaviors?" The truth is: neither and both. The child is doing kind behaviors because it is in the nature of the child to be kind. We can apply the label "kind" because that is the label we use for such actions, but the actions are proceeding from the child's nature, before the child even knows what kindness is.

This inadequate example may help illuminate my point about God. God has a nature that is moral; by that I mean inherent in God's nature are values and ethics. I have assigned human words—*good* or *right* as distinct from *evil* or *bad*—to these values. Those values and morals that reflect the nature of God are good. We can observe these (1) as taught to us in revelation, (2) as lived in the life of the incarnated God and (3) as sensed by us because we are made in the image of God.

Taught in revelation. First, I return to the idea of law in the Bible. In the laws God reveals his nature in a particular human culture at a certain time of history. These laws show people to be poor reflections of God's innate character because no one is up to the task of living like God. As Paul says, no one is good and no one does a good deed in light of God's purest state. This is similarly borne out by the teachings of Jesus. When the Pharisees came to probe Jesus' teachings on divorce they asked whether it was lawful to divorce, "for any cause." Jesus responded, "What God has joined together, let not man separate." The Pharisees then asked why God gave a law through Moses that provided for a certificate of divorce. Jesus responded that the law was not a perfect expression of God's character; rather, God was trying to salvage the best from the lives of imperfect humans. As Jesus said, "Because of your hardness of heart Moses allowed you to divorce your wives, but from the beginning it was not so" (Mt 19:3-9).

Scripture sets forth God's moral nature as the purpose of the atonement. In the Old Testament a time of repentance and sacrifice was set aside for the annual Day of Atonement. The sacrifice on the Day of Atonement was for the sins of the people, recognizing that God is a moral God. God established a teaching process where the sins of the people were symbolically placed on a goat, which was driven out from the midst of God and his people (Lev 16). That God is a pure and moral being in his very essence is woven throughout Scripture, starting with the expulsion of the sinful Adam and Eve from the Garden. The expulsion confirms that God cannot dwell in fellowship with anything that is less than pure. Paul follows the same theme through his writings.

In the letter to the church at Rome, Paul distinguishes our unrighteousness from God's righteousness. People need justification, to be made righteous, for eternal fellowship with God. The sacrifice of Christ offers real atonement, in contrast to the symbolic atonement set out in the Old Testament. Paul is emphatic that the atonement was necessary for the sins of everyone, those who died before Christ just as much as for those who die afterward (Rom 3:23-26). The key to understanding the atonement is to first understand that God is by nature a moral being. As such, his relationships of fellowship (unity as opposed to enmity) must conform to his moral character. In the atonement God satisfied this need in an appropriately just way to enable permanent fellowship between him and his people. None of this is necessary if God is not at his core a moral being.

Lived in the incarnated God. The incarnation of Jesus has moral implications. Because Jesus is God clothed in humanity, we can see in his actions the actions of God. We see good and righteousness perfectly exemplified in human life. We see the morality of God in Jesus' life. As Jesus told his apostles, "Whoever has seen me has seen the Father" (Jn 14:9). Before Jesus was arrested and crucified, he prayed to God about his coming ordeal.

> And now, Father, glorify me in your presence with the glory that I had with you before the world existed. I have manifested your name to the people whom you gave me out of the world. . . .
>
> O righteous Father, even though the world does not know you, I know you. . . . I made known to them your name. (Jn 17:5-6, 25-26)

In Jesus we see God's nature, and the actions of Jesus are the actions of God. In this sense we can see the limitations in Euthyphro's dilemma. Jesus is not good because he did good things. Neither did Jesus do the things he did because he was determined to do good deeds. The deeds of Jesus are done out of the very nature of God. Those deeds are "good" or "righteous" because they are manifestations of God's character.

Sensed by image bearers. One of the more profound lessons of Scripture relevant to the issue of right and wrong is found in the references to people as made in the image of God (Gen 1:26-27).

This distinguishes humans from the animal world. Only Adam and Eve are made in God's image. Humanity possesses a unique similarity to God. Genesis 2 provides more detail as Adam tried to find a proper companion among all the creatures made by God. No other animal was suitable, so God made Eve, another person created in God's image. While these passages do not explore fully what it means to bear God's image, Genesis quickly links it to ethics in the next few stories. In the Noah story God specified that killing innocent people is wrong because they are made in God's image.

There is in each person an ingrained morality that is a reflection of the morality of God. To be sure, the image is marred and in some it is distorted beyond recognition. Yet for most there is a sense of right and wrong that exists, even though it is hard to explain, define or justify. This imprint of God's morality is carried by those made in his image.

Morality is not some objective right or wrong that God either does or instructs others to do (á la Euthyphro). The Bible sets forward God as a moral being who makes choices consistent with his moral character. The values and acts consistent with God's essence are what we properly term "good," "right" or "moral." Those values contrary to God's nature we properly term "evil," "wrong" or "immoral." Thus God neither conforms to nor invents the moral order; rather his very nature is the standard.

Not surprisingly, then, traditional Jewish and Christian thinkers have dismissed Euthyphro's dilemma as inapplicable to God. Jewish scholars Ari Sagi and Daniel Statman criticize Euthyphro from an Old Testament perspective.[13] From the Christian perspective Katherine Rogers notes: "Anselm, like Augustine before him and Aquinas later, rejects both horns of the Euthyphro dilemma. God neither conforms to nor invents the moral order. Rather his very nature is the standard for value."[14]

Someone might fairly ask, "So what? Does this really matter?" Absolutely. All moral choices and values must be based on something. It might be one's instinct, what makes one happy, what seems to be the best for most people, what someone has taught or maybe something else. Regardless, there is an end of the line that explains or justifies what we think is right or good. Christians believe the end of the line is God. Right or good is what God's character calls for. Any other end source or determining factor will not uphold what is really good and right.

THE IMMORALITY OF HITLER AND THE MORAL GOD

I began this chapter by asking whether we can fairly call Hitler's actions good or evil. Most everyone is quick to say that murdering innocents is wrong. Yet when pressed on how they know, some will argue it just is wrong, as if everyone else should agree. Of course, the wrongness of such an atrocity is plain to those made in God's image. But curiously, many people will not credit the rightness or wrongness of a deed to deity. Others will judge Hitler's actions wrong because they did not benefit society or they violated the values of the majority. We saw earlier, though, that these arguments are inadequate. Deciding what is right and wrong and imposing that on others boils down to where the end of the line is. Do people determine right and wrong themselves, or do they have a fixed point outside of themselves that serves as the standard for right and wrong.

CONCLUSION

Christians believe the actions of Hitler were clearly wrong and evil. Hitler violated the character and nature of God as he killed those made in God's image. God has communicated the truth of his character in revelation (the Bible), in incarnation (Jesus) and intrinsically (in his image bearers). These give meaning and direction to the inherent moral compass we carry. They are sensible and recognizable sources for right and wrong. For centuries a measuring rod kept in Paris defined a meter. That rod was originally thought to mark one ten-millionth of the distance between the North Pole and the equator. This, the metric-using world agreed, would be a "meter." From this rod other metric measurements (millimeter, kilometer, etc.) drew their meaning and specifications. Without some agreed standard, *meter* could mean one thing to one person and something different to another. This is a good example of the dilemma of human morality.

The biblical teaching removes relativism from core morality. There is a measuring rod found not in Paris but in God. With it we can answer questions of the morality of human trafficking and more.

Last week, I took the deposition of the owner of a chain of strip joints, places he calls "gentleman's clubs." I took the case because of the facts; here is a wrong that cries out for justice.

A patron of the club, whom I will call John, went in at 9:15 p.m. on "two dollar Tuesday," so named because all drinks were two dollars apiece. The law says a club is not allowed to serve anyone who is intoxicated and that an intoxicated person is not allowed to leave the club without another driver (or the club is to call and pay for a taxi). The legal definition of intoxication is a blood alcohol level of 0.08.

The club has video cameras recording everything, so we have a second-by-second account of what happened. John went in and drank his first beer by 9:21. John had a second beer and a tequila shot by 9:28. Over the next three hours, John had at least thirteen beers and six tequila shots. The video showed him clumsily knocking over bottles, having trouble standing and acting inappropriately. The end came when John was unable to pay the twenty dollars for his most recent lap dance. The dancer complained to the manager, who then approached John.

Once the manager discovered John had spent his last dime and had no more money for liquor or dancing, he escorted John to the door, making him leave the club—but not before letting John chug his last beer.

John staggered out the door, past the valet chair and got into his car. Six minutes later John was driving 130 miles an hour down a freeway in the dark of night without his lights. John smashed into the car of Emily, an eighteen-year-old who was headed home from a friend's house, killing her instantly. Remarkably, John survived. He was taken to a hospital where they finally took his blood-alcohol level three hours after his last drink at the club. He was 0.29, not only over three times the legal limit but above the level that can prove fatal (0.25).

As I deposed the owner of this club, my first question was, "How many people have died as a result of alcohol served in this club?" His answer was three, until I pointed out he had forgotten one; the true answer was four. In his mind, he ran a business. He traded in sex and alcohol, and the only real question for him was how much money he made.

I will take this case to a jury to find out if this is right or wrong by our community standards. But I do not need a jury to tell me whether it is right or wrong. I have a better measuring rod—God.

As for those who might play Socrates and ask us whether God is good because he does good or whether good is good because God commands it, the Christian can readily respond that God's nature is itself the ultimate standard of good. God is the end of the line.

9

Free Will, Moral Responsibility and the Infinite, Just God

I DON'T DO CRIMINAL DEFENSE WORK. It is important work, and the innocently accused need access to good, competent criminal attorneys, but it is something I have no desire to do.

One of America's most famous criminal defense lawyers of the last one hundred years was Clarence Darrow. His fame came from not only representing high-profile people but also in the way he handled their cases. In his famous defense of confessed killers Nathan Leopold and Richard Loeb, Darrow's clients avoided the death penalty through a strategy that became legal lore.

Rather than defend his clients, Darrow attacked society. He put on evidence about his clients' childhood. He showed their abusive parents, the destructive neighborhood where they grew up and the horrible circumstances that "made the men." Darrow combined this horrendous background with certain physical traits like his clients' mental capacity and painted a picture of fate and determinism. Today we would say he argued that genetics and environment, rather than human choice, determined their behaviors.

This approach resonated with the judge and the public. After all, as Darrow asserted in his twelve-hour closing argument, the defendants really had no choice; their lot in life was cast, and they were not to blame.

When the trial concluded, the judge denied the state's request for the death penalty, providing an appropriate setup for the subject of this chapter.

Having examined the issues of God's limits and identity, of revelation and communication, of what is real, and of the moral nature of God, I now turn our examination to people. Can a person make true moral choices? Are people free to decide one way or another, or are their choices predetermined? This issue I examine through the following witnesses:

Witness List

B. F. Skinner (1904–1990). *Perhaps the twentieth century's most influential psychologist, B. F. Skinner held a PhD from Harvard University, where he subsequently taught, holding the Edgar Pierce Chair. He was well known as an author and social philosopher.*

Noam Chomsky (1928–). *In this chapter I recall Professor Chomsky to the stand. His description is found in chapter six.*

St. John the Apostle. *In this chapter I recall John to the stand. His description is found in chapter five.*

St. Paul. *In this chapter I recall Paul to the stand. His description is found in chapter four.*

BEYOND FREEDOM AND DIGNITY

In 1971 B. F. Skinner, the Edgar Pierce Professor of Psychology at Harvard University, published the popular book *Beyond Freedom and Dignity*. In the slim paperback Skinner set out a "technology for behavior" that he considered long overdue. The book emphasized basic principles that would justify and explain how to modify the behavior of humans. Some saw the book as the academic follow-up to George Orwell's *1984*, where a few were selected to mold and shape the behavior of the masses. Skinner's desire to see one part of humanity manipulate and control the behavior of another part is itself disturbing. What is equally provocative are the premises that underlie Skinner's beliefs about behavior modification.

Skinner was a determinist. He believed that all the actions of every person are preset and determined. He thought that science had finally advanced to a point of recognizing that everyone is determined by genetics and environment (see fig. 9.1). For Skinner, every thought, every decision and every action does not proceed from a free will or an autonomous being. Instead, the DNA of a person, interacting with environmental factors, produces every mental and physical change or action. Our brains, the seat of actions in the body, are a pool of chemicals and matter that respond to the laws of chemistry and physics. Skinner believed that these laws always dictate how the chemicals and molecules of the brain act and interact. He thought that as assuredly as two plus two is always four, the laws of the universe dictate a person's decisions and actions.

Figure 9.1. B. F. Skinner (Wikimedia Commons)

Think of it in everyday terms. Why are you reading right now? If I put the question into a cause-and-effect analysis, your reading these words is the effect. What has caused you to read these words? Skinner would not accept the answer "It was my choice." For Skinner, making a choice is an illusion; you really have no choice, at least as that word is generally used. Instead, you have a genetic makeup that enables you to read, you have been in environments that have taught you to read, and you have come to this point in your life where this material has interested you enough to at least read to this point. Those interests were stirred by other environmental factors that have affected you. The causes behind each effect go back beyond our ability to analyze or verbalize. Skinner believed that given the world as it is—the environment that has subsumed you (the values that you were taught, the positive reinforcement you received when certain things happened, the negative reinforcement received when other things happened, etc.) and your genetic makeup—if he could rewind the tape, you would make the choice to read this book every time. There would be no difference, for you really never made a choice. Your brain chemistry and the molecular reaction to the environmental stimuli would always have the same result, just as assuredly as the laws of chemistry and physics are inviolable.

The belief that a person has an attitude, a sense of responsibility, concerns and a will for this or that were anachronisms to Skinner. These were really nothing more than quaint ideas from a prescientific time. Today we know the genetic makeup of the brain and outside stimuli (the environment) have set up chemical chain reactions in the brain. The charade of nonphysical things like ideas and choices are in fact predetermined chemical reactions that are no more open to change than the rule that two plus two is four. Skinner asked where "such nonphysical things as purposes, deliberations, plans, decisions, theories, tensions, and value" come from. He noted that prescience views might indicate they came "from the gods, or God," but he considered such an answer unacceptable in our scientific age. His answer had only two sources: "A person's genetic endowment, a product of the evolution of the species, is said to explain part of the workings of his mind and personal history the rest."[1] Skinner wrote dismissively of the idea that people were autonomous beings with a free will. It is prescientific. "Autonomous man serves to explain only the things we are not yet able to explain in other ways. His existence depends upon our ignorance, and he naturally loses status as we come to know more about behavior."[2]

There are some readily appreciable yet disturbing consequences of Skinner's beliefs. Skinner does not run from these but rather embraces them. He readily concedes that people should not be credited when they do something right. Similarly, no one can be held "responsible for what he does," nor can one be "justly punished" in the sense of a real responsibility.[3] As the title of the book forecasts, Skinner believed science had moved and was continuing to move human understanding of behavior into a mechanical process where "nothing is eventually left for which autonomous man can take credit."[4] Science was on a course to destroy the idea of everyone's dignity and freedom. For Skinner, we are machines, albeit biological ones.

In chapter eight I discussed right and wrong, and Skinner's approach to morality was similarly mechanical, turning the terms on their heads: "To make a value judgment by calling something good or bad is to classify it in terms of its reinforcing effects."[5] By this Skinner set out his subjective view of right and wrong in terms of the ultimate goal of his book. Skinner wanted people to use his beliefs to sculpt the environment for the good of humanity. By positively reinforcing behaviors that are desirable (give treats), and negatively reinforcing the undesirable ones (mete out punishments), the world could become what Skinner thought it should become. Behavior could be dictated.

Even the most ardent supporter of free will should pay attention to what Skinner has proposed. Skinner was not some fly-by-night fellow with a handy pen and a good publisher. In a 2002 survey Skinner was selected as the most eminent psychologist of the twentieth century; Sigmund Freud was third.[6]

Skinner's approach is not novel, and philosophers have debated for thousands of years what measure of free will, if any, people possess. Skinner did not engage the philosophical debating points. To him philosophy held less weight than what is learned through science. Philosophers have generally divided those who argue about free will and determinism into three broad camps (see fig. 9.2).

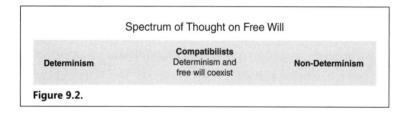

Figure 9.2.

As noted earlier, Skinner was a determinist. The determinist camp has been divided into subgroups, often termed hard and soft determinists, and the precise definition of *determinism* can vary from author to author. The ultimate idea is that at any point in time the state of the world, which includes humans, is already determined solely by an earlier state of the world and the laws of physics. Put more simply, the past combined with the laws of physics provide every truth of the future (see fig. 9.3).

At the other end of the spectrum are those who believe determinism is false. Typically, although not necessarily, these people believe in free will. As a general definition, *free will* means the human capacity to choose a course of action from among various alternatives. This might seem simple enough; however, even it is divided into various camps. Plato, for example, believed that people have three aspects to their souls that are responsible for actions. Only the higher "rational" part of the soul had free will (as opposed, for example, to the appetite and its more base decisions). From this perspective the changes from the state of things in A to that in B is the result of not only the laws of physics but also the choices of humanity.

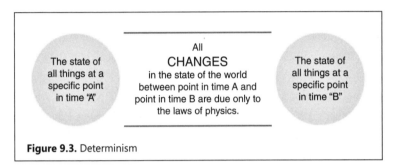

Figure 9.3. Determinism

Some of the most interesting debates among philosophers have stemmed from the middle camp, the *compatibilists*. This viewpoint accepts some tenets of determinism, yet also allows for the exercise of free will.

Much of the concern over meshing determinism with free will arises from the need to assess moral responsibility. As Darrow asked in the Leopold and Loeb trial, can we hold a person morally responsible for taking an action if that person is not free to choose another action? The following are some reasons that make free will important:

- Without free will, how can we be truly responsible for our actions?

- Without free will, what truth is there in words of praise for another's efforts, courage or creativity? If the person is simply reacting chemically and has no choice in his or her actions, then such praise is meaningless.

- Without free will, we cannot have any measure of dignity over any other aspect of nature. There is nothing special about being just another cog in a machine.

- Without free will, what value is there to the love we have for another? Similarly, what value is there in friendship? Love is simply one set of chemical reactions to another's chemical reactions.

So, we have Skinner's scientific approach and the philosopher's approach to free will and determinism. Neither has a consensus of support. Each year brings new assessments of earlier views. Skinner's science has received scathing reviews like that of Noam Chomsky: "Since his William James lectures of 1947, Skinner has been sparring with these and related problems. The results are nil. . . . No scientific hypotheses with supporting evidence have been produced to substantiate the extravagant claims to which he is addicted."[7] After pointing out that science does not prove what Skinner asserts, Chomsky quotes Skinner's fallback position that "as the science of behavior progresses, it will, inevitably, more fully establish these facts." Chomsky tells the other side of such speculations: "At the moment we have virtually no scientific evidence and not even the germs of an interesting hypothesis about how human behavior is determined."[8]

In the decades since Skinner and Chomsky wrote, science and technology have developed a number of different tests to determine whether a person is motivated to act and then the brain processes a decision to act (generally deemed consistent with determinism) or whether the decision to act precedes the motivation. The results and interpretations of these tests vary greatly. Viewpoints are all over the map.

If we accept the premises established in our earlier chapters, then we are in a different place on this issue. Scripture has revealed that people are bearers of God's image. God did not make us mere machines. We have the ability to choose that makes us morally responsible. In a moral sense as well as an artistic sense, the Bible claims we are creators made in the image of the Creator. The Bible teaches that God makes true choices. His actions are not determined by anything other than his own character. Genesis portrays God as deciding to create the world and all that is in it. This was God's choice, exercised in his Godness. It also proclaims man and woman as made in God's image.

This makes humanity free to act and choose as well. We can make moral decisions (as well as houses, clothes and things more typically associated with the word *create*). We are not unlimited like God. For example, I have DNA, and it has determined the color of my hair. I can be creative and choose to dye my hair, but I am only making a choice about what color my hair appears to be. I have not changed my DNA, and over time its real color will grow back. Similarly, I was able to choose my college degree in biblical languages, but I did not choose to be born into a family where education and college were priorities.

Therefore, the biblical view places people in the camp of those who believe humans can make real choices and be held morally accountable for those choices. It does not remove the influence of heredity and environment, but it does not make those fully determinative of all actions. Philosphers would categorize it as "compatibilist."

Does the biblical explanation comport with common sense? In a courtroom two elements come into play. First, what evidence is there? We do have unquestionable evidence that DNA plays a role in our lives. It affects our physical features, including many features of our brains and their functioning. We also know, and most everyone readily accepts, that our environment shapes our behaviors, attitudes and actions. I am reminded of the experiments of Ivan Pavlov (1849–1936), who consistently fed his dog after ringing a bell. After a time, his dog would begin salivating when hearing a bell (classical conditioning). Yet science does not end there; we have the testimony of those like Chomsky who point out that these two factors are not the sole determiners of human behavior.

The lack of evidence leads us to consider common sense. Do we really believe that people have no choice in life? Of course a jury composed only of B. F. Skinner and his followers would say yes, but I suggest the vast majority would not. In their gut most everyone will agree that they make choices. They know they can choose one road or another. They think about decisions and try to contemplate what to do. We see this clearly on the cover of Skinner's book.

Of Skinner's book the *New York Times* trumpeted, "If you plan to read only one book this year, this is probably the one you should choose!" Note the irony of this endorsement: "If you plan to read . . . this is the one you should choose" (see fig. 9.4). I contend that

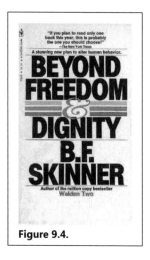

Figure 9.4.

the biblical teaching that humans, within limitations, are truly able to choose is not only a truth borne out by science but also by experience and common sense.

WHERE DOES GOD FIT INTO THIS DEBATE?

Even beyond the immediate question of whether we can make choices, these issues have deeper implications. They properly turn our minds to the concept of cause and effect.

In our observations of the universe and our own lives we experience firsthand that events have readily traceable causes. On a fundamental level, for example, these words are readable because I entered them onto a computer keyboard. From there they were transferred to a printer or perhaps to another computer. The printer produced written copies, which were then distributed in such a way that one came into your possession. Of course, we can trace these causes to much deeper levels. For example, we could add that the keyboard I used was attached to a microprocessor that turned each keystroke into computer language. Each of those levels can again be reduced further, and much like dividing fractions into smaller fractions, the process is almost unending. This process must have some starting point, but that starting point ultimately would not be found until reaching the start of the universe. From there, the debate can commence about who or what started the universe.

As we think through this, it should not come as a surprise that people have been writing and thinking about causality for thousands of years. Aristotle categorized causes. Many thinkers since have refined and defined causes into types, orders of occurrence and ways we perceive them. Causality is the warp and woof of the universe's fabric. Humans experience a consistent cause-and-effect universe. According to the laws of gravity a heavy item always drops from the table rather than floating to the ceiling.

Because we live and experience cause and effect 24/7, there always are traceable reasons for everything. The roll of the dice? We might say they deliver chance results, but in truth the way the dice were held, the force they were thrown with, the rotation, the wind, the surface for landing—all these things cause the resulting position.

Why do we experience cause and effect? More importantly, are these so pervasive that through the laws of physics everything can be traced back to the beginning of the universe? Are the determinists right? Are we cogs in the cause-and-effect machinery of the world? Is there no real moral responsibility because no real choices are made?

The biblical answer is unequivocally no. We do live in a cause-and-effect world, but the Bible teaches that humans choose behaviors and ideas. These choices become one of the causes. People are autonomous, albeit with limitations. People are responsible for their moral choices.

Free Will and the Bible

Free will *is not a biblical term; it is a term of philosophers. Some philosophers define it in such a way that not even God has free will! For example, God is not free to sin. As discussed in chapter seven, by definition sin is what God does* not *do. The biblical concept of autonomous choice, commonly termed* free will, *is that people are free to act within their nature. Everyone's freedom has certain constraints. I am not free to make myself a frog simply because I decide to.*

The world as we perceive it is recognizable and makes logical sense if we consider that (1) we are a finite people who (2) live in a finite universe created where (3) laws of consistency in cause and effect exist. Consider each element of this idea.

We are a finite people. Humans have limits, both physically and chronologically. We exist in a particular space. I am here, not here and somewhere else at the same time. I may tell my wife, "I may be out of town, but my heart is still at home." But what I really mean is that I miss her. We also exist in a time. I am here today, but I was not here one hundred years ago. Similarly, there will come a time when I, as I exist right now in this body with these thoughts and limitations, will not exist, absent some intervening miracle of God. Our finite limitations are not only in areas of space and time. We are limited in what we know, limited in what we can do, limited in our relationships. In one sense we are defined by our limitations.

The limits of who we are and what we think define where we end and the outside begins.

We live in a finite universe. There are limitations in the things around us. We can see where this line begins and ends. While the night sky seems to stretch on forever, we know that it is not unending. In objective experience, everything we experience and touch, everything that is physical in the universe, is finite. Now some will say, "But the universe did not arise from nothing, so the universe is unlimited in time." However, this derives not from observation but the presuppositions of the people arguing. Some cannot imagine anything without a cause or beginning and are content with assigning the beginning of things, while others never want to credit something or Someone with starting or creating a universe.

Laws of consistency in cause and effect exist. We live in a universe of consistencies that enable us to learn and live. For example, airplanes fly because the air flowing over the wing is moving faster than the air flowing under it, which results in lower pressure above the wing. The wing (and the plane) moves toward the lower pressure. This is not magic; it is an expression of a consistent principle of moving gases and fluids. It is the result of the core truth of the consistency of cause and effect.

Contrast our ideas of people and the universe with God. God is different than a human in that God is infinite. The finite universe and its laws of consistency in cause and effect reflect an important aspect of God's nature. God is not human; infinite God does not have anyone's limitations. He is not a supersized version of a person. He is not just a stronger, longer-living collection of material substance that has greater powers. God is God, and much greater in form, substance and ability than anything anyone can ever ponder.

There is a difference between bearing the image of another and being identical to that other. My son bears an image or resemblance to me. Many of our features and personality traits are remarkably similar. Yet we are certainly different people with different limitations and features. As image bearers of God, we are similar to him, yet there are distinctions as well. People share the moral values of God's moral nature. A noteworthy distinction between people and God is that we are finite and God is not. God is infinite. He does not have our limitations. God is not limited by space or time. We do not find God in one place to the exclusion of another, nor do we find him existing at one time but not another.

Thousands of years ago the psalmist remarked on this profundity in a very personal and practical manner. Psalm 139:7-12 proclaims God's infinite presence in space.

Where shall I go from your Spirit?
    Or where shall I flee from your presence?
If I ascend to heaven, you are there!
    If I make my bed in Sheol, you are there!
If I take the wings of the morning
    and dwell in the uttermost parts of the sea,
even there your hand shall lead me,
    and your right hand shall hold me.
If I say, "Surely the darkness shall cover me,
    and the light about me be night,"
even the darkness is not dark to you;
    the night is bright as the day,
    for darkness is as light with you.

The same psalm recounts God's infinite presence in time. God is not limited to the here and now of each moment unfolding.

Even before a word is on my tongue,
    Behold, O LORD, you know it altogether. . . .

Your eyes saw my unformed substance;
in your book were written, every one of them,
  the days that were formed for me,
  when as yet there was none of them.
How precious to me are your thoughts, O God!
How vast is the sum of them!
If I would count them, they are more than the sand.
  (Ps 139:4, 16-18)

God has existence not only in the universe but also outside of it. He is the infinite beyond. Understanding this, many people begin to see God as the ultimate cause. This has an element of truth, but it is not fully accurate. This debate quickly unfolds into a discussion of whether that makes God the source of evil. (Two related questions for discussion center on whether God could have made a better universe and whether salvation is a matter of predestination.) Here, we need to integrate the picture between God and us. While God is infinite, we are not. While God is morally perfect, we are not. These pieces of the puzzle fit together and form a whole only if certain other pieces are added. The key piece that gives this puzzle definition is our ability to make choices.

What is at stake? I suggest the answer lies deep within us. If we do not have the ability to make real choices, we escape responsibility for our misdeeds. We can play the mental games like, "Yes, I know I should not have a temper, but that's just the way I am." Or "Yes, I should avoid pornography, but I succumb to it because I am wired that way." If, on the other hand, we have the ability to make choices, then our poor behavior takes on a new light. This is not to say that DNA and environment play no role, for they certainly do. These can make us more prone to one sin or another. But we must realize that choice plays a very significant role.

Scripture teaches that though finite, every person bears God's image and has the ability to choose and effect change. As image bearers we are, in our limited space and time, creators. God is not the source of evil, unless *source* is used in the limited sense of God being the source of humans who were created with the ability to choose evil. We are a true cause in the chain of cause and effect.

The apostle John had a revelation while on the island of Patmos. That revelation included letters written to seven churches, including the church in the Asia Minor town of Laodicea. The letter speaks of the works of the church. These were not predetermined actions, they were choices made by the church that were not aligned with God's will: "I know your works: you are neither cold nor hot. Would that you were either cold or hot!" (Rev 3:15). The choices being made were deliberate and optional. The people could choose: "Behold, I stand at the door and knock. If anyone hears my voice and opens the door, I will come in to him and eat with him, and he with me" (Rev 3:20).

How do we exercise these choices? Where does the choice come from? How do we understand it in light of the chemistry of the brain and the laws of nature? Some think it may actually be a physical process, not yet discerned by science, that fosters the ability to make nondetermined choices. Earlier I referenced MIT's Noam Chomsky's critique of B. F. Skinner. Chomsky questioned whether science might unfold such a truth: "Suppose that in fact the human brain operates by physical principles (perhaps now unknown) that provide for free choice, appropriate to situations but only marginally affected by environmental contingencies."[9]

Scholars have long known that some things can be proven by affirmation while others are best known by negative proof. In other words, sometimes we need to build our understanding of things by eliminating what they are not. Because our DNA and the environment are causes in how we think, it does not mean that they are the only causes. Even within the confines of the contributing causes of genetics and environment, real choices can be made. For example, I have the genetic ability to process the proteins from a fillet of fish, and I have experienced how tasty the fish can be when prepared properly, therefore I might choose to eat it. However, these causes do not preclude the fact that I choose to eat it or not. These causes intermingle and work together.

The Bible reveals not only the ability to choose but also the moral responsibility that corresponds to that choice. If we return to the letter to the church at Laodicea, we see that the church embraced the world's riches rather than the riches of God's will in their lives: "For you say, I am rich, I have prospered, and I need nothing, not realizing that you are wretched, pitiable, poor, blind, and naked" (Rev 3:17). John urges them to think through their decisions and make a different choice: "I counsel you to buy from me gold refined by fire, so that you may be rich, and white garments so that you may clothe yourself and the shame of your nakedness may not be seen, and salve to anoint your eyes, so that you may see" (Rev 3:18).

Paul similarly addressed people's choices. They could choose to "walk by the Spirit" or to gratify the "desires of the flesh." Christians are free to make those choices. "For you were called to freedom, brothers. Only do not use your freedom as an opportunity for the flesh, but through love serve one another. . . . But I say, walk by the Spirit, and you will not gratify the desires of the flesh" (Gal 5:13, 16).

Jesus also spoke of the human will, distinguishing the choices of people from those of God. As Jesus looked on the city of Jerusalem, about to enter it and meet his death, he exclaimed, "O Jerusalem, Jerusalem, the city that kills the prophets and stones those who are sent to it! How often would I have gathered your children together as a hen gathers her brood under her wings, and you were not

willing!" (Mt 23:37). John, Paul and Jesus referenced real choices
made by real people. People are not simply machines following their
predetermined paths with no independent or autonomous choices
in the matter. They bear moral responsibility for their choices.

The laws of consistency in cause and effect reflect an important
aspect of God's nature. Paul wrote to the Roman church that God's
character is expressed in creation: "His invisible attributes, namely,
his eternal power and divine nature, have been clearly perceived,
ever since the creation of the world, in the things that have been
made" (Rom 1:20). Everything made exhibits consistency, especially in cause and effect. In Hebrews we read that Jesus Christ, "the
radiance of the glory of God and the exact imprint of his nature"
(Heb 1:3), is "the same yesterday and today and forever" (Heb 13:8).
This consistency is also seen in God's nature. God does not tolerate
impurity or immorality. In Romans 1 Paul explains that many have
chosen a course of ungodliness, walking contrary to the nature and
morality of God. He identifies the effects of this ungodly course of
action. Paul says "God gave them up" to impurity, to dishonorable
passions and to a debased mind. "Claiming to be wise," these
people "became fools." God's "righteous decree" is that people who
did such things "deserve to die" (see Rom 1:18-31).

It is remarkable that many today do not understand why God
holds sinners accountable. They see a world where actions always
have consequences, yet they fail to see the goodness and wisdom
of God's reliability and consistency. Cause and effect necessitate
condemnation and death for the immorality and impurity that run
rampant among humanity. In Romans 2:2 Paul says that "the
judgment of God rightly falls on those who practice such things."
The question for humanity is whether there is a way out of the
moral death trap, out of what Paul in Romans 8:2 calls "the law of
sin and death"?

CONCLUSION

Something in us screams "I have a choice." This is the reason we instinctively hold people accountable for bad deeds. B. F. Skinner attempted to dislodge human freedom and dignity, but his scientific and logical shortcomings and unprovable presuppositions have been exposed by thinkers such as Noam Chomsky. We are not predetermined machines without moral responsibility. We make real choices. There is something about us that is autonomous and free. As such, we have true moral responsibility for the choices we make. The truth and consistency of cause and effect confirm the revelation of Scripture that God must address sin and unrighteousness in a just and consequential manner. Exactly how God has done so is the subject of chapter ten.

10

The Audacity
of the Resurrection

"USE YOUR COMMON SENSE." It is a plea heard every day in courtrooms around the country. Fair, well-informed people are able to sift through mountains of evidence and use common sense to form opinions and make decisions. I seek to bring common sense to this chapter as we proceed further in our examination, focusing on the issue of a bodily resurrection of Jesus as fact or fiction.

If we accept the reasonable conclusions about God's power and nature, about his communication to humanity, about the true moral nature of sin and the human accountability that comes with the power to choose, we then must explain how the pure God can relate to sinful humanity. The Christian answer is the death and resurrection of Jesus Christ. Can reasonable people accept such an audacious claim?

Witness List

St. Matthew. *In this chapter I recall Matthew to the stand. Matthew's description is found in chapter six.*

St. John the Apostle. *In this chapter I recall John to the stand. John's description is found in chapter five.*

St. Paul. *In this chapter I recall Paul to the stand. Paul's description is found in chapter four.*

St. Peter (1st century A.D.). *Peter was an apostle famous for defending Jesus on the night of his betrayal, but then denying him soon thereafter. Peter was an eyewitness to the empty tomb as well as to the resurrected Jesus.*

St. Mark (1st century A.D.). *Mark was an early Christian missionary, serving for a time with Paul and Barnabas. The early church recorded that Mark (also known as John Mark) wrote his Gospel from information he received from Peter while in Rome.*

St. Luke (1st century A.D.). *Luke was a first-century physician and a missionary companion of Paul's. He talked to a number of eyewitnesses to the events around Jesus' life, death and resurrection, as well as the early historical events surrounding the church.*

Polycarp (A.D. c. 70–c. 156). *One of the early church martyrs who died for his belief in the resurrected Christ is Polycarp, the second bishop of the church at Smyrna (modern-day Turkey). We know of Polycarp through letters written by him and to him, early narratives written about him (by Irenaeus and the early church historian Eusebius), as well as the detailed account of his death,* The Martyrdom of Polycarp.

Titus Flavius Josephus (A.D. 37–c. 100). *Josephus was a Jewish military leader in Jerusalem's first-century rebellion against Rome. After capture, he became a loyal Roman subject composing, among other things, a history of the Jews.*

Publius (or Gaius) Cornelius Tacitus (A.D. 56–117). *Tacitus was a Roman senator and a historian. Among his writings are histories of his day.*

Gaius Suetonius Tranquillus (A.D. c. 70–post 130). *Suetonius served as director of the Imperial Archives under the Roman* *emperor Trajan, who ruled from 98 to 117. Later, Suetonius was the personal secretary to the Roman emperor Hadrian (119–121). During this time he wrote a history of the lives of the Caesars, finishing it around A.D. 119.*

Gaius Plinius Caecilius Secundus, better known as Pliny the Younger (A.D. 61–c. 112). *Pliny the Younger was a lawyer, author and Roman magistrate. As part of his professional duties, he wrote a number of letters that have survived to this day.*

Charles Colson (1931–2012). *Chuck Colson served President Richard Nixon as special counsel and admitted guilt associated with the Watergate break-in, serving a seven-month prison sentence. After his crime Colson converted to Christianity and became a well-known Christian leader and cultural commentator.*

In this chapter I want to subject the resurrection of Christ to the rigors and standards of the judicial system and see what reasonable conclusion is best drawn from the evidence. As best as I can, I want to determine what happened to Jesus of Nazareth. Before doing so, I am going to set out certain important legal concepts and rules for guiding jury decisions. These rules are designed to eliminate jury mistakes in the jury's role as the "finder of facts."

TRIAL RULES AND PRINCIPLES

Juries are charged with making their decisions based on evidence. *Direct evidence* comes mainly from witnesses and documents. Additionally, juries are allowed to look at *circumstantial evidence*, which is evidence that is reasonably inferred from the facts. As we look at the principles associated with juries and the evidence they consider, I should emphasize that there is more than we can put into one chapter. Still, the following is a good core overview of what is built into the jury system to make it arguably the most effective determiner of historical fact in civilization.

Witnesses: Credibility. Some of the witnesses are *fact witnesses*, which means they actually saw or witnessed something relevant firsthand. Other witnesses are *experts* who are generally paid to give their expert opinion on a matter that is better understood with specialized information not readily known by the common person. The jury is charged with the responsibility of determining the credibility of witnesses.

The determination of credibility can entail many things.[1] Among the important indications of credibility are

- *The mental condition of the witness.* A mentally unstable or challenged witness is generally less likely to be accorded credibility. Jurors will look for witnesses who seem convinced of their testimony, who will look the jurors in the eyes, who are ready and willing to give their testimony without fear of it being heard or documented. Some witnesses are determined mentally challenged to such a degree that they are not allowed to testify.

- *The witness's motives.* For some witnesses the motive may be as simple as telling the truth. For others, especially expert witnesses, there is often an economic consideration. Some witnesses are paid for their testimony, which typically detracts from its credibility. Similarly, some witnesses have a personal stake in the outcome (e.g., a defendant who might have to go to jail, a plaintiff who might win money or a defendant who might lose money).

- *Comparison of different witness accounts.* Frequently, juries are faced with multiple witness accounts to the same set of facts. In that circumstance credibility often hinges, at least in part, on the relative merits of one person's testimony versus that of another. A weighing process can be involved, and when four witnesses agree on some issue or another, each witness's credibility is enhanced by the testimony of the others.

- *The character of the witness.* This is a very powerful influence in the credibility decision of jurors. So much so that there are very strict rules about what character evidence can be offered about witnesses. For example, if a witness has a reputation for dishonesty and there is evidence of such, then certain rules apply as to how and where that testimony can be offered. Clearly, a pathological liar will have less credibility over against an honest witness.

Witnesses: Hearsay testimony. As a general rule, fact witnesses are only allowed to testify to what they witnessed firsthand. The idea that a witness might say "John told me that he saw ABC" is not deemed testimony that ABC happened. It is merely testimony that someone else said he or she saw ABC. In courtroom vernacular this is called hearsay, which is when a witness asserts that what he or she "heard said" (the root of "hearsay") accurately related certain facts. Courts have recognized that once the factual examination includes statements of what others have said, a second layer of remoteness affects the strength of the comment. There are numerous exceptions to the inadmissibility of hearsay, often based on whether the original speaker ("the declarant") is available to offer the testimony firsthand. For example, if the first speaker is not available to testify, then the statements of that speaker are admissible to a jury if they were given in another trial or proceeding, or if the declarant thought his or her death was imminent in some way related to the statements. Very importantly, if the first speaker's statements are contrary to his or her healthful pursuit of life (including effects to one's economics, liberty, etc.), then the hearsay comments are admissible.

Expert witnesses: Junk science. Experts, generally paid witnesses in a case hired by one side or another, are allowed to testify to opinions arising from the expert's particular knowledge, skill, experience, training or education. These opinions are allowed before a jury if based on sufficient facts or data, and if reliable principles and methods are applied to those facts to justify the opinions. This is the Daubert rule discussed in the preface. Courts have continually refined this rule to make certain that jurors are not handed *junk science*, the term applied to far-reaching opinions that have no real basis in reality. In a trial the judge is the gatekeeper of whether an expert's testimony is both relevant and adequately based on science. There are multiple factors the court considers in making this determination. The core concern is whether experts have an economic motive behind their opinions, which might move some beyond the realm of what is reasonably real and into the realm of the speculative.

Bias, sympathy and prejudice. Jurors are instructed not to make decisions based on bias, sympathy or prejudice. In fact, those whose biases, sympathies or prejudices are deemed too strong to be set aside are removed from consideration for serving on a jury.

Burden of proof. No trial is conducted based on the idea that jurors can be 100 percent certain of the facts. Determining the past is not a scientific or mathematical matter like determining whether the Pythagorean theorem is right in claiming $A^2 + B^2 = C^2$. Math and science have a certainty that comes from dealing with truths of the universe's physical laws. That is not the same as determining historical truths. As I have already noted, there is always the miniscule chance that reality as we see it is not real (e.g., we are dreaming or in a computer program). To seek a mathematical proof for the reality of a historical fact is like using a liquid form of measurement to determine distance. It is senseless to say "my house is three gallons from the store" or "I drank two miles of water." Similarly, it is senseless to talk of proving a historical event by mathematics or laboratory experiments.

The courtroom determines historical fact using the "burden of proof." One side or another has an obligation or burden to prove something as true or false. That burden fluctuates, depending on the matters in controversy. If the issue is a criminal matter, where someone's liberty will be stripped away by a contrary finding, then the burden of proof is "beyond a reasonable doubt." The approach is that we cannot strip away a person's life or liberty unless the finder of fact is convinced of the truth of a case "beyond a reasonable doubt."

In civil cases—for example, where person A brings a claim against person B for driving while drunk, causing a wreck and injuring person A—the party required to prove their case must do so by "the preponderance of the evidence." This means that the question for the jury in finding facts is simply "what is more likely than not?" These burdens are important aspects of jury trials because 100 percent certainty is never reachable in any case. It simply is not an option in historical fact reconstruction.

Certainly, there are other factors that have been left out of this consideration. Jurors are generally listening to advocates who present opposing sides to a historical situation. Although there are exceptions, jurors are generally not allowed to question witnesses themselves. Trials do not even occur until there has been a time of "discovery" in which witnesses are examined to see what they have to say, facts are uncovered and documents are examined. This is when expert witnesses are retained and where arguments are marshaled for presentation.

Armed with these factors, I can now turn to the resurrection of Jesus, asking, What really happened? This is the most important finding of fact right we will face. So, let's consider the question with civilization's best tools.

THE RESURRECTION OF JESUS

The witnesses to the death and resurrection of Christ are numerous. I will place them in categories as we consider the main points of their testimony.

Direct eyewitnesses. Matthew. The writer of the First Gospel was an apostle, one of Jesus' select Twelve. Originally a tax collector, a job that required not only writing skills but also careful and good record keeping, Matthew was called by Jesus from the tax collector's booth to be one of his disciples. The details of this calling are given only in Matthew's Gospel (Mt 9:9). Matthew's Gospel records Jesus' crucifixion, death, burial in the tomb of Joseph of Arimathea, the Roman guard at the tomb, the earthquake and the resurrection. The resurrection account includes the direct testimony of two women (Mary of Magdalene and a second woman named Mary) about what they saw and their inspection of the tomb. It also includes an apparently common explanation why the body of Jesus was missing from the tomb: the Jewish elders gave money to the soldiers to tell people that his disciples stole the body (Mt 28:11-15).

John. Along with his brother James, John was a fisherman who was called to leave his nets and follow Jesus (Mt 4:21-22). His account, the Fourth Gospel, details Jesus' last speech to his apostles, in which Jesus explained he was leaving but assured them he would return. John repeats the prayer Jesus offered in Gethsemane before his arrest, where Jesus affirmed his preexistence with God, his mission on earth and his oneness with God the Father. John then details the betrayal and arrest of Jesus, the confrontation with the Jewish authorities, the denial of Peter, the trial of Jesus before Pilate and the crucifixion. John very carefully explains that Jesus died on the cross, with nail holes in his hands and feet and a spear thrust into his side. John tells of the role of Joseph of Arimathea as well as the Jewish ruler Nicodemus in the burial of Jesus in Joseph's tomb. John attests to the empty tomb by Mary Magdalene, the follow-up tomb inspection by Peter and, most scholars accord, by John himself (he does not call himself John but "the other disciple, the one whom Jesus loved"). Peter and the other disciple saw the burial clothes and the otherwise empty tomb. John records visits of the resurrected Jesus to Mary Magdalene and the disciples. John also records the encounter between the resurrected Jesus and the apostle Thomas, at which time Thomas at first doubted, wanting to see and touch Jesus and his wounds. Once the resurrected Jesus offered Thomas that very opportunity, Thomas's doubts immediately disappeared. Jesus made subsequent postresurrection appearances documented by John, including one where Jesus cooked and ate a fish-and-bread breakfast with his disciples on the shore of the Sea of Galilee. Jesus prophesied that Peter would die by crucifixion and that John would be the last living apostle.

Paul. An eyewitness of a different sort, Paul was raised in a devout Jewish home, was one of the Jewish elite (educated in the highest and best Jewish academic environment), was fluent in at least Hebrew, Aramaic and Greek, knew Greek poetry, was a multigenerational Roman citizen conversant with Roman law, and was a zealot among his people, living above reproach by Jewish law and tradition. Paul was part of the Jewish power structure that was violently against the church, seeking to arrest and, if need be, kill those who were trumpeting Jesus as a resurrected Messiah. A follower of Jesus named Stephen, the first known martyr of the Christian faith, was stoned under Paul's approval (he held the cloaks of those involved). While Paul was on a zealous crusade ravaging the church, hauling both men and women to prison, he had an encounter with the risen Jesus while on the road to Damascus. Jesus identified himself to Paul and instructed him on what to do to resolve the blindness Paul suffered as a result of this encounter. Paul almost immediately began preaching Jesus as the risen Messiah, recounting his encounter with the risen Jesus multiple times. Throughout much of the Mediterranean world Paul proclaimed that God had raised Jesus from the dead (Acts 17:31). In his writings to the Corinthians, Paul specifies that "Christ died for our sins in accordance with the Scriptures, that he was buried, that he was raised on the third day in accordance with the Scriptures, and that he appeared to [Peter], then to the twelve" (1 Cor 15:3-5). Paul adds that the resurrected Christ appeared to over five hundred disciples at one time, with most of them still alive lest anyone should want to check. Finally, Paul affirmed that the resurrected Jesus appeared to Jesus' brother James and to Paul.

Peter. Like John, Peter was a fisherman called to follow Jesus. After Jesus' arrest, for fear of his own safety Peter denied being Jesus' associate three times in rapid succession. Ultimately, according to the Gospel writers, Peter not only encountered the empty tomb but also the risen Jesus. In one of his own writings, Peter spoke of the resurrected Jesus as "a lamb without blemish or spot. He was foreknown before the foundation of the world but was made manifest in the last times for the sake of you who through him are believers in God, who raised him from the dead and gave him glory, so that your faith and hope are in God" (1 Pet 1:19-21). Peter also wrote of his assurance that the resurrected Jesus would return with a new heaven and a new earth (2 Pet 3).

Secondary witnesses. Mark. According to historical records of the church, the missionary Mark, who worked under Paul, Barnabas and Peter, penned the Second Gospel (the Gospel of Mark). Early historical church records report that Mark received his Gospel information from Peter. That would make Mark's Gospel hearsay in legal theory, which means it would not be admissible in a court absent certain indications of reliability. Saving admissibility issues for later, I note now that Mark's account does confirm the crucifixion and death of Jesus. He also details the burial and involvement by Joseph of Arimathea. Mark recorded that on the Sunday following the crucifixion Mary Magdalene and Mary the mother of

James found the tomb empty. An angel informed both women that Jesus was resurrected. The earliest copies of Mark's account end there. Later copies include appearances of Jesus to Mary, to two disciples and also to the entire group of eleven remaining disciples.

Luke. Luke wrote the Third Gospel as well as the book of Acts. Luke was not an eyewitness of the Gospel events, but he set out to "compile a narrative" from "eyewitnesses" (Lk 1:1-2). He then set out to write "an orderly account" (v. 3), which includes the early history of the church in Acts. Periodically in the Acts narrative Luke joins Paul on mission efforts, and his writing then includes eyewitness accounts. Luke explains not only the plot to kill Jesus but the events that led up to the crucifixion. Luke recounts the drama before the actual crucifixion, including the difficulties carrying the cross to the site of Jesus' death. In addition to Jesus' death, Luke adds the burial by Joseph of Arimathea, providing details about Joseph's role as a member of the Jewish council and his objection to the killing of Jesus. Luke details the story of the women coming to the tomb and finding Jesus' body missing. He adds to Peter's investigation of the empty tomb his discovery of Jesus' linen clothes. Luke gives many more details than the other Gospel writers about Jesus' postresurrection appearances, including walking with two disciples on the road to Emmaus, showing the disciples in Jerusalem his wounds and eating some broiled fish the disciples had with them. At the end of that encounter, Jesus explained to the disciples the Old Testament's teaching about his death and resurrection. He finished with the assurance they would receive the Holy Spirit. Luke ends with Jesus' ascension into heaven (see Lk 24).

Note that Luke identifies his sources for those who might want to confirm the accounts. Luke, for example, not only identifies Matthew's two women witnesses but adds another element, "the other women." And while Matthew identifies the two women as Mary

Magdalene and "the other Mary," Luke says, "Mary Magdalene and Joanna and Mary the mother of James."

Early church martyrs. There are many other witnesses relevant to Jesus' death and resurrection, including a group of early church martyrs. These people gladly laid down their lives, convinced that Jesus, the resurrected Messiah, assured them of the reality of God, of sin, of atonement and of a better life after this one is over.

While I could list enough of these witnesses to create a separate book simply with their testimony, I present only one to see the ancient accounting of this witness's words and actions. My exemplar witness is Polycarp, whose martyrdom is set forth in *The Martyrdom of Polycarp.*[2]

Because Polycarp was wanted for his faith and was a leader of the church, the believing community hid him in the countryside. Those searching for Polycarp found two slave boys that, after being tortured, told the authorities where Polycarp was hidden (6.1). So the mounted police and horsemen set out to find and arrest this old Christian man. Polycarp had enough warning to escape, but opted to stay, saying, "May God's will be done" (7.1).

Upon hearing that the police had arrived, Polycarp started visiting with them. Those present were amazed not only at his advanced age but also at his composure in the face of what was to come. Polycarp ordered that his captors be given the supper they must have missed by chasing him at that hour. Polycarp also asked his captors for permission to pray for an hour before they left. The captors agreed, and to everyone's wonder, he stood for two hours, praying out loud for everyone "who had ever come into contact with him" (7.2–8.1).

His captors and those with them regretted coming after "such a godly old man" (7.2), but they still took him into the city. There the police captain and his father attempted to persuade him to state

"Caesar is Lord," followed by an offering of incense. They explained that Polycarp could return to business as normal and live if he would do those two minor things. Polycarp responded, "I am not going to do what you are suggesting to me." Then Polycarp went straightway into the stadium where the crowd noise rose so high that "no one could even be heard" (8.1-3).

Polycarp and the Christians with him heard a voice from heaven as he entered the stadium: "Be strong, Polycarp, and act like a man." Then the proconsul asked Polycarp whether he was indeed the legendary and wanted man, which Polycarp confirmed. The proconsul then tried to persuade Polycarp to recant, urging Polycarp to "swear by the genius of Caesar." Thinking of the Christians as atheists (for not believing in the deity of Caesar and other gods of the Roman pantheon), the proconsul asked Polycarp to say "Away with the atheists!" So Polycarp "solemnly looked at the whole crowd of lawless heathen who were in the stadium, motioned toward them with his hand, and then said, 'Away with the atheists!'" Not quite what the magistrate intended!

The magistrate cried, "Swear the oath and I will release you; revile Christ." To this Polycarp responded, "For eighty-six years I have been his servant, and he has done me no wrong. How can I blaspheme my King who saved me?" (9.1-3).

The proconsul kept at Polycarp with wave after wave of persuasion and offers to save his life by recanting his faith. But Polycarp never faltered. Instead, Polycarp explained, "If you vainly suppose that I will swear by the genius of Caesar, as you request, and pretend not to know who I am, listen carefully: I am a Christian. Now if you want to learn the doctrine of Christianity, name a day and give me a hearing" (10.1-2).

As the proconsul moved into the final stage of confrontation, Polycarp was filled with courage and joy, and his face was "filled with grace." Even the proconsul was astonished. Meanwhile, the crowd itself was emphatically shouting and chanting for Polycarp's death. The cries eventually turned into demands that Polycarp be burned (12.1-3).

As they started to nail Polycarp to the pyre, he stopped them: "Leave me as I am; for he who enables me to endure the fire will also enable me to remain on the pyre without moving, even without the sense of security you get from the nails" (13.1-3). So instead of nailing Polycarp, they tied him up. Polycarp looked to heaven and offered a prayer of praise to God testifying to God's love through Jesus. And as Polycarp declared "Amen!" the fire was lit (15.1).

And "such is the story of the martyrdom of Polycarp" (19.1). Many everywhere spoke of his death, "even by pagans" (19.1). Early in the 200s, the Christian writer Tertullian said that the blood of the martyrs was the seed of the church. More and more people were inspired and further convinced by a faith that people would gladly die for, than by the paganism that would kill those believers.

Other witnesses. In addition to the early church writings there are historical writers like Josephus, who wrote Jewish history for the Romans. Around A.D. 93–94, Josephus wrote of the martyr James, who was identified as "the brother of Jesus, who was called Messiah [Christ]." He also said Christ was executed by Pilate. Josephus has more to say about Jesus as resurrected.

At this time there was a wise man called Jesus, and his conduct was good, and he was known to be virtuous. Many people among the Jews and the other nations became his disciples. Pilate condemned him to be crucified and to die. But those who had become his disciples did not abandon his discipleship. They reported that he appeared to them three days after his crucifixion and that he was alive. Accordingly, he was perhaps the Messiah, concerning whom the prophets have reported wonders. And the tribe of Christians, so named after him, has not disappeared to this day.[3]

In addition to Josephus other Roman historians wrote of Jesus as the subject of worship among Christians. In his *Annals*, penned around A.D. 116, Tacitus wrote of the July 64 mass execution by Nero (see fig. 10.1). Tacitus confirmed the death of Christ by crucifixion ("the extreme penalty") under Pilate as arising from Nero's efforts to distract attention from his burning of Rome:

Figure 10.1. Gaius Cornelius Tacitus (Wikimedia Commons)

To get rid of the report, Nero fastened the guilt and inflicted the most exquisite tortures on a class hated for their abominations, called Christians by the populace. Christus, from whom the name had its origin, suffered the extreme penalty during the reign of Tiberius at the hands of one of our procurators, Pontius Pilatus, and a most mischievous superstition, thus checked for the moment, again broke out not only in Judaea, the first source of the evil, but even in Rome, where all things hideous and shameful from every part of the world find their center and become popular.[4]

Even before Tacitus, another Roman, commonly called Pliny the Younger, who was both lawyer and author, served for a time as a magistrate for the Roman emperor Trajan and wrote about Jesus and Christians. In his capacity as magistrate Pliny pursued Christians for their illegal status within the empire. Pliny explains the Christian practice of meeting on "a fixed day" (which scholars readily accord would have been Sunday, the resurrection day) and

partaking of a meal (the Eucharist). He adds that he made a point
of following policy and executing those who would not recant.[5]

In his *Lives of the Caesars*, Suetonius, the Roman emperor's
director of the imperial archives, used those archives to write of
the significant events of the empire's Caesars. Suetonius wrote
that during the reign of Claudius (41–54), the Jews in Rome were
constantly having disputes over Christ, which reached an in-
tensity level so high that Claudius expelled the Jews from Rome
for some time.[6] This event is also referenced in the New Testament
(Acts 18:2).

Witnesses: Credibility. We do not have the ability to judge the
credibility of these witnesses by looking them in the eye and focusing on their demeanor. Instead, we can examine their writings
and the writings of others about them. In some ways those writings
convey more relevant information on credibility than a two-hour
examination might. The writings have been subject to near ex-
haustive analysis over the last nineteen centuries.

The mental condition of the witnesses. No scholar has produced a
credible argument that these witnesses are mentally challenged or
deranged. The writings of Paul, for example, are lucid and exhibit
well-reasoned logic, marvelous command of language, some of history's most moving prose (1 Cor 13), profound theology (Phil 2:5-11),
knowledgeable confrontation of those with whom he disagreed (Gal
2:11-14), and more indications of mental stability and competence.

The witnesses' motives. Not one witness among the many listed
could be seen as having an economic motive for subscribing to or
supporting the resurrected Christ. In fact, the opposite is true.
Christianity was not supported in Judea. Early believers in the resurrected Jesus faced persecution and death at the hands of Jews.
The faithful Jews, including Paul before his conversion, believed
that God had sent their forefathers into exile because they tolerated

gods other than the God of Moses. The idea of a resurrected Jesus who was God and Savior would only bring trouble to Judea from the hand of the true God, or so they reasoned. Were they not truly convinced, the apostles and disciples of Christ (almost all of which abandoned him at the cross) would not sanely abandon their faith for a renegade idea about a resurrected Jesus. Furthermore, if they were charlatans who trumped up the idea of a resurrection, then you would not expect Peter, who denied the Lord three times in an effort to save his skin, to stick with the hoax once he faced imprisonment and death. The stoning of Stephen alone would have likely brought a faked resurrection to an end.

Closely considering the motives of Paul, we see something striking. Paul was a "Who's Who" among the Jews. Having studied under Gamaliel, a teacher of the Jewish law so famous that many of his sayings are extant today, Paul was in a position to lead the Jews. He cast his vote to stone Stephen (Acts 7:58; 26:9-10). Paul zealously adhered to Jewish laws. Paul lost his affluence, position, standards and practices of life, and likely his family when he converted. He certainly was convinced that something tremendous happened in Jesus.

Paul knew what he had traded for. He wrote as much to the believers in Corinth, explaining that if Christ has not been raised from the dead, then Christianity is a cruel joke (1 Cor 15:19).

History records that Paul, Peter, Thomas and most every other apostle eventually died a martyr's death out of their deep conviction that Jesus rose from the grave. Every one of the apostles exhibited a 180-degree turn in life and lived the rest of their days adhering to faith in the living Christ. The only motive was a firm belief in the truth of the resurrection.

Does history indicate these witnesses believed for profit or fame? No. There was no profit for Paul, Peter, James, Stephen or any others associated with Jesus. Nor was there fame (at least not in their lifetime). To the contrary, it made them outcasts and cost them their positions. Paul, by his own accord, suffered "countless beatings, often near death." Five times he received forty lashes from the Jews. Three times he was beaten with rods. Once he was stoned. Three times shipwrecked. He chose a life in "danger from robbers, danger from my own people, danger from Gentiles, danger in the city, danger in the wilderness, danger at sea, danger from false brothers; in toil and hardship, through many a sleepless night, in hunger and thirst, often without food, in cold and exposure" (2 Cor 11:26-28). He preached "free of charge" (2 Cor 11:7) and worked as a tentmaker to support himself in ministry. Finally, history records, Paul willingly died a martyr's death at the hands of Nero rather than budge on the truth of the resurrected Jesus.

Stephen was martyred around A.D. 34 because he would not deny the truth of the resurrection (Acts 6–7). The apostle James (demarcated in the New Testament as "the brother of John") was martyred around A.D. 44 because he would not deny the truth of the resurrection (Acts 12). A later historical record, written 125 years after James's death by Clement of Alexandria, notes that James's accuser listened to his confession of faith and was so moved that he became a believer and was also martyred for his faith.[7] A different James in the New Testament was "the brother of Jesus" (Mk 6:3), who did not believe in Jesus during Jesus' ministry (Jn 7:1-5). Yet after the resurrection we read of James being among the believers (Gal 1:19). James the brother of Jesus was thrown from the parapet of the temple and clubbed to death because he refused to deny the resurrected Jesus. Hegesippus, writing A.D. 170, records that James was pushed off the parapet because a number of watching Jews were moved to faith by his testimony.[8] The apostle Andrew was hung on a cross for four days before finally dying. He chose the misery and impending death rather than deny the truth of the resurrection.

Did the apostles risk life and limb for the fame of starting a movement? This motive likewise fails. It is readily apparent from reading the witnesses that they all believed that Jesus was soon going to return to take them to a glorified state. Believers in Christ were selling all their goods to support the common good in light of what they thought was around the corner (Acts 2:44).

Comparison of different witnesses' accounts. In my courtroom experience, anytime two stories are identical, there is a strong likelihood of collusion. The truth is that eyewitnesses notice different things. One may see two cars racing through an intersection while another notices a green one. That does not mean one is right and the other wrong. It means that the stories need to be combined to see if they make sense.

Much has been made over whether the biblical eyewitness accounts are consistent. On core matters they certainly are. Only on minor matters are different facts presented, none of which undermine a coherent narrative. All of the accounts include (1) the crucifixion of Jesus, (2) his death on the cross, (3) his burial in the tomb of a noteworthy citizen who could be examined for the truth, (4) his resurrection on the third day and (5) witnesses to the empty tomb. Matthew, Luke and John also name witnesses who encountered the physically resurrected Jesus.

The character of the witnesses. Honesty is a virtue, but it is not always easy to tell when it exists. There is an expression that people need to "put their money where their mouth is" to prove their conviction. This reveals honesty. Each of the eyewitnesses put more than their money where their mouth was. They gave all they had for their convictions about the resurrected Jesus.

Another way to consider the character of the witnesses comes from the circumstantial evidence (see "Opening Statement" in chap. 1). Each of the eyewitnesses lived full and real lives. They had family and friends who knew their penchant for truth telling or the lack thereof. These eyewitnesses successfully proclaimed Jesus' resurrection to such an extent that within two decades it had spread throughout the Roman Empire, becoming a legal religion by 313 and the official religion of the empire by 380.

Witnesses: Hearsay. The testimony of Matthew, John, Paul and Peter is not hearsay. They were eyewitnesses to what they recorded and to what they said. A court would consider Mark's and Luke's writings hearsay.[9] They were not eyewitnesses but recorded the information they received from others. Before a court would allow consideration of their testimony, it would need to meet an exception to the hearsay doctrine. Some of the testimony, however, would be accepted in a court of law. For example, testifying before King Agrippa, Paul began, "I consider myself fortunate that it is before you, King Agrippa, I am going to make my defense today" (Acts 26:2). His testimony included doing "many things in opposing the name of Jesus" (Acts 26:9), which we have looked at earlier in this chapter. This testimony of Luke, as a recorded trial, is admissible as a recorded judicial proceeding.

Of course, all the statements of the noneyewitnesses would be hearsay as statements "against interests." At that point in history, everyone proclaiming Jesus as the resurrected Lord was doing so under threat of imprisonment or death. The stoning of Stephen bears that out.

So regarding hearsay, it is not an issue for the testimony about Jesus' resurrection according to Matthew and Luke, and where it is, it fits into exceptions that push the testimony into a realm of reliability.

Expert witnesses: Junk science. There are no hired experts or anyone who is testifying to the resurrection for pay. However, science is an important area to consider, for some will say, "Yes, based on the eyewitness accounts there is more than sufficient evidence to believe in a resurrected Jesus, but we know that scientifically it is impossible. So there must be another explanation."

I begin this discussion by readily admitting that absent God intervening in the laws of physics, it is not rational to believe in resurrection, anymore than we should believe two plus two is ten. The same principle that two plus two is four, however, sets the resurrection onto firm logical ground. Science says there is no resurrection by the rules of this universe. A resurrection could occur if and only if there is someone or something that can operate outside of the laws of this universe. That is true of God. God is not some molecular entity bound by matter. God is not so small. God is beyond the universe and is able to alter things in the universe. That is the only way science can allow for the resurrection. Science dictates the necessity of God's involvement, unless all these witnesses were massively deceived and wrong.

Bias, sympathy and prejudice. Who gets to be a juror on the resurrection case? Of course, everyone does. Everyone must confront the issue of whether or not they see the hand of God in the life, death and resurrection of Christ. Even though everyone gets to be a juror, I still need to address the issue of bias, sympathy and prejudice. Because some might get disqualified from sitting on an actual jury if this were a real case in court.

Consider two different groups that would not likely be allowed on a jury. First, there might be a group that says, "I believe! I don't care what the evidence is. I have a prejudice and bias that Jesus was resurrected. I was born into it; it is genetic. It must be the truth, and I could never examine it genuinely." This person has a bias that would preclude jury service. That is not to say that the person is wrong. Many people can be right in their opinions but are not allowed to sit on a jury.

The second group says, "I cannot set aside my prejudice about the laws of nature. A resurrection is a functional impossibility. It doesn't matter if fifty thousand people saw it, those fifty thousand must be deceived." This person does not have an open mind, even to the idea that God can do what is impossible for people and molecules. These people still have to make a decision, but they are fooling themselves if they think they are making a rational one based on the evidence. They are making it based on their bias and prejudice. The evidence becomes irrelevant and not worth listening to or examining.

Burden of proof. We end with the burden of proof. As noted in the legal section, no one can be 100 percent convinced about any finding of fact in history, especially so far back in time. The question then becomes what standard of proof we would need before trusting in a conclusion that Jesus indeed suffered under Pontius Pilate, was crucified, died, was buried, descended to the dead and on the third day rose again. Is the burden of proof what is more likely than not, like a civil case? Is it beyond a reasonable doubt, like a death penalty case?

Under either burden the evidence for a resurrected Jesus is immensely compelling. We have looked at that evidence from eyewitnesses and secondary witnesses, but I have left out some of the greatest arguments. The death and resurrection of Jesus are the missing piece of the puzzle in this book. Christ's death allows a just God to set aside the immorality and impurity of humanity and accord humanity a resurrection into perfection, just as Christ was resurrected.

This is the beauty of the finished work of Christ. His last words, "It is finished," reflect the atoning work that the nature of God requires. Here we see not only the records and testimony of the witnesses to the resurrected Christ but the logic and meaning behind it. It was not some harebrained idea concocted by a few fishermen, a tax collector and a budding rabbi that somehow caught fire amid a dreadful and documented persecution, finally arriving three hundred years later as a legal religion. It was the facts—no more and no less. It was prophesied for centuries in Scripture, and it was fulfilled in history.

Was the Missing Body of Jesus and the Following Testimony One Big Conspiracy?

Charles Colson, the assistant to President Richard Nixon who was convicted in the Watergate scandal, writes:

> *Watergate involved a conspiracy perpetuated by the closest aides to the president of the United States—the most powerful men in America, who were intensely loyal to their president. But one of them, John Dean, turned state's evidence, that is, testified against Nixon, as he put it, "to save his own skin"—and he did so only two weeks after informing the president about what was really going on—two weeks! The cover-up, the lie, could only be held together for two weeks, and then everybody else jumped ship in order to save themselves. Now, the fact is that all those around the president were facing embarrassment, maybe prison. Nobody's life was at stake.*
>
> *But what about the disciples? Twelve powerless men, peasants really, were facing not just embarrassment or political disgrace, but beatings, stonings, execution. Every single one of the disciples insisted, to their dying breaths, that they had physically seen Jesus bodily raised from the dead. Don't you think that one of those apostles would have cracked before being beheaded or stoned? That one of them would have made a deal with the authorities? None did. Men will give their lives for something they believe to be true; they will never give their lives for something they know to be false.*

> *The Watergate cover-up reveals the true nature of humanity. Even political zealots at the pinnacle of power will, in the crunch, save their own necks, even at the expense of the ones they profess to serve so loyally. But the apostles could not deny Jesus, because they had seen him face to face, and they knew he had risen from the dead.*[10]

No one lives up to the revealed instructions or moral purity of God, whether in the commands of Scripture or revealed in the life of Jesus. Sin could be the end of the story for each of us were it not for God's provision and plan found in the work of Jesus. Paul taught the Ephesians that through Christ God was "making known" to the church "the mystery of his will."

In the fullness of time God planned to "unite all things in [Christ], things in heaven and things on earth" (Eph 1:10). This was never a "Plan B" for God. Unlimited by time, God planned it before the foundation of the world. It was an act of love: taking on flesh as a perfect man, only to die a cursed sinner's death. This was not done capriciously; it was the solution to humanity's immoral choices. Through Jesus' life, death and resurrection everyone could find the release from the death they deserved because of their sin. The death of Christ was attributed to sinners outside of time. I say "outside of time" because that is the way of God.

God operates in this universe, and in that sense operates in time. Yet God exists infinitely and eternally, outside of the universe and outside of time. In this sense God was able to pass over the sins of Abraham and others who died before Christ's atoning death, crediting them with the forgiveness that would come through Christ. Paul explained to the Romans that Christ's death was necessitated because of sins committed before his incarnation. In this way, the death of Christ showed "God's righteousness, because in his divine forbearance he had passed over former sins" (Rom 3:25).

How does this happen? How is the death of Christ applied to a person? Here is the audacity of the resurrection. God acted outside of nature, outside of space and time, and resurrected Jesus Christ from the dead. He performed a miracle that would not happen short of divine intervention. After dying a sinner's death, Christ was resurrected as the God of power he was from eternity. The grave could not hold a perfect man. Because of his faithfulness to the Father, Jesus had the power of an indestructible life. Death had no power over the One who is life. This was and is the key for human hope. While we are human, we have an alternative to the death demanded by our sinfulness. We have a way into God's purity.

Paul explained to the Ephesians that God, "even when we were dead in our trespasses, made us alive together with Christ—by grace you have been saved—and raised us up with him" (Eph 2:5-6). The resurrection of Christ is the key for us. We are made alive with him. God acted out of his great love for us (Eph 2:4). This is not something anyone earns or achieves on his or her own. It is God's free gift enabled by the cross of Christ and the empty tomb, apportioned to us through our faith and trust (Eph 2:8-10).

This is indeed the work of a mighty God.

11

Death and Eternity

A COMMON COMPLAINT of the American courtroom is that it feeds a "lawsuit lottery" mentality. The idea is that people with nothing to lose file a fake lawsuit hoping to beguile a jury into a lottery-esque verdict, or hoping to use the courtroom threat to leverage an undeserved settlement.

As I have noted before, juries can get it wrong, but that is incredibly rare. Furthermore, when they do, it is so obvious that appellate courts readily overturn those verdicts. Those of us close to the system affirm that a person has a better chance of collecting from a real lottery than from a game of "lawsuit lottery."

For many, the idea of heaven and an afterlife is similar to the lottery. It is not something they think they will win, but they still want it. In this chapter we examine the reasonableness of an afterlife and eternity.

Witness List

Jesus of Nazareth. *As God incarnate, crucified and resurrected, Jesus forms the foundation of the Christian faith, both today and for eternity.*

St. Paul. *In this chapter, I recall Paul to the stand. Paul's description is found in chapter four.*

THE BIBLE AND COMMON SENSE SEE HEAVEN AS A DESTINY, NOT A LOTTERY

There are many things that people hope for that do not have a substantial chance of happening. The statistical likelihood of winning a single state lottery is generally recognized as 1 in 18 million. To give some measure of perspective to these odds, in a single year the odds of being murdered in America are 1 in 18,000. In other words, if you were to buy one lottery ticket this year, then you are a thousand times more likely to be murdered than you are to win the lottery. If you buy a lottery ticket for the United States Powerball game, then your odds are 1 in slightly over 80 million. You are one hundred times more likely to drown in the tub than you are to win the Powerball lottery. You are three times more likely to be attacked by a bear than you are to win with that lottery ticket. And the odds of dying in a car wreck on your way to buying the ticket would scare you into walking (until you saw the odds of getting hit by a car while walking).[1]

Even with these statistical truths, one out of two Americans is believed to have bought a lottery ticket. They are driven by the hope of winning, even in the face of insurmountable odds. After all, we read about people winning. We can all play the game of "What would I do if I won the lottery?" This feeds our hope and desire, bringing many to the point of purchasing. The optimists often feel lucky. Pessimists or realists are not tempted to buy the ticket. These people realize that to increase the odds of winning Powerball would require buying a ticket each year for eighty years over one million lifetimes. That is a long time to wait for odds to even out.

For many people the idea of heaven and eternal life is not much different than a lottery. Life consists of what they see and have, and if there is something beyond this life, well and good. But heaven is at best a pie-in-the-sky dream, which might or might not be there.

Faith may be useful in the world, perhaps even as down payment on a lottery ticket for eternity. However, heaven is a cherry that will top this life, not a confident expectation after death. Some who hold this view are generally cynical of anything they cannot verify. For others, though, it comes from a humility that does not want to presume on God.

To people who are not confidently expecting heaven or eternity, I suggest the following maxim: "If your God cares about you only in this world and only in your life, then your God defies common sense."

HOW DID WE GET TO THIS CHAPTER?

This book did not start with this chapter, and for good reason. Before we discuss eternity, it is necessary to see the reasonableness of believing in a personal, moral and infinite God who has communicated with people. Furthermore, we need to understand that people make real choices. Yet all too often they choose immorality. Jesus' death is the solution to sin. Subsequently, he was resurrected and he ascended to heaven.

There is nothing small about a God who plans and accomplishes such things out of his love for people. But does it end there? Is this life all there is? Can we be confident that the future holds anything concrete for us? Paul has much to say about this. He explained to the Ephesians that the reason God has done these things is not simply to make us better people on earth. God raised us up with Christ "and seated us with him in the heavenly places in Christ Jesus, so that in the coming ages he might show the immeasurable riches of his grace in kindness toward us in Christ Jesus" (Eph 2:6-7).

The future is not determined by a lottery; it is a destiny in Christ.

WHAT DOES THE FUTURE HOLD?

Heaven has various meanings. It has multiple meanings in the Bible.

Heaven sometimes refers to the skies and space. This is the "expanse" of Genesis 1—the place of the stars and where birds fly. *Heaven* is also used as a term for the dwelling place of God. This is the heaven "above the stars" (Is 14:13). Jesus taught his disciples to pray to God as "our Father in heaven" (Mt 6:9). Repeatedly, God is noted as being in heaven or being our "heavenly Father" (Mt 6:26, 32; 7:11, 21). This is where God's will is done (Mt 6:10) and is the term used for God's eternal kingdom (Mt 7:21; 10:7).

As the word is used for God's dwelling outside of space and time, it is where the redeemed reside beyond this life. "Abraham, Isaac, and Jacob" recline at a table "in the kingdom of heaven" (Mt 8:11). And we are to direct our efforts toward heaven, as Jesus taught his disciples: "Do not lay up for yourselves treasures on earth, where moth and rust destroy and where thieves break in and steal, but lay up for yourselves treasures in heaven, where neither moth nor rust destroys and where thieves do not break in and steal" (Mt 6:19-20).

Do God's children "go to heaven" when they die? What is our future? Paul addresses the Corinthians on this. First, after setting out the many witnesses to the resurrection of Christ, he discusses the implications of the resurrection for Christians. Then, Paul explores what the resurrection of the dead entails. I will follow both trains of thought here.

The implications of Christ's resurrection. Paul wrote to the church in Corinth because some Christians apparently denied the future resurrection of the dead (1 Cor 15:12). Paul's message was direct and blunt. He began a hypothetical statement to test the ramifications of their beliefs: "If there is no resurrection . . ." (v. 13). He finishes this hypothetical with multiple responses. For Paul, no resurrection means

- Jesus was not resurrected. (v. 13)

- Paul's preaching was in vain. (v. 14)

- The faith of believers was in vain. (v. 14)

- Paul was misrepresenting God. (v. 15)

- The Christians' faith is futile. (v. 17)

- Everyone is still in his or her sins. (v. 17)

- The dead are gone. (v. 18)

Paul concludes, "If in Christ we have hope in this life only, we are of all people most to be pitied" (v. 19). New Testament scholar Gordon Fee applies Paul's concerns to today:

> To deny Christ's resurrection is tantamount to a denial of Christian existence altogether. Yet many do so to make the faith more palatable to "modern man," we are told. But that will scarcely do. What modern man accepts in its place is no longer the Christian faith, which predicates divine forgiveness through Christ's death on his resurrection. Nothing else is the Christian faith, and those who reject the actuality of the resurrection of Christ need to face the consequences of such rejection, that they are bearing false witness against God himself. Like the Corinthians they will have believed in vain since the faith is finally predicated on whether or not Paul is right on this issue.[2]

Paul then examines the implications of affirming Christ's resurrection. Resurrection means

- Christ was resurrected. (v. 20)

- Resurrection comes to those in Christ. (v. 22)

- Christ will come again and eventually destroy even death. (vv. 24-26)

Fee explains,

> The resurrection of Christ has determined our existence for all time and eternity. We do not merely live out our length of

days and then have the hope of resurrection as an addendum; rather, as Paul makes plain in this passage, Christ's resurrection has set in motion a chain of inexorable events that absolutely determines our present and our future.[3]

This was not a lottery issue for Paul. The resurrection's implications are both profound and mandatory. It is a critical part of the work of God in Christ.

Paul knew his teaching would likely not answer the objections of those who doubted the resurrection from the dead. Having explained why the resurrection was a theological imperative, Paul now turned his attention to the objections of those in denial. It is clear from reading Paul's entire discourse in 1 Corinthians 15 that he was confronting opposition to the idea that life would come back to a corpse. Death was final. They could not imagine how resurrection could occur. Paul explains that no matter how spiritual the Corinthians considered themselves, their concept of God was inadequate.

HOW CAN THERE BE A RESURRECTION? WHAT WILL IT BE LIKE?

Paul sets out the likely verbal challenge of those who opposed his resurrection teaching: "But someone will ask, 'How are the dead raised? With what kind of body do they come?'" (1 Cor 15:35). They could not wrap their heads around the visible reality that dead bodies decay; they do not reanimate.

Paul responds harshly to these people, calling them foolish. They were fools in the sense that they did not take God into account (see Ps 14:1). Paul then uses everyday occurrences to make his point. He points to seeds, which also go into the ground and decay. The seed's decay does not end the life cycle but opens the door to the seed's potential as a new plant in a new form (1 Cor 15:36-38). In this sense death does not thwart God's design; it is a critical part of it.

Just as the body of a seed is transformed into the body of a plant, and just as the body of a caterpillar is transformed into the body of a butterfly, so it will be, Paul explains, for the resurrection body. We do not know in molecular terms what the resurrection body will be. Nor do we know what it looks like. What we do know are the ways that the resurrected body will contrast with the body of this life in this world (see table 11.1).

Table 11.1. The Natural Body Contrasted with the Resurrected Body

Body of this Life	Body of the Resurrected Life
Perishable (Subject to decay)	Imperishable
Dishonorable (A body of humiliation)	Glorified
Weak	Powerful
Natural	Supernatural

Paul sets out the resurrected body in sharp contrast to the natural body. It is not subject to the frailties of this life. It is fit for the eternal kingdom of God (vv. 42-49). Paul adds that flesh and blood of this universe cannot exist in God's eternity. The body must become imperishable to dwell in the imperishable kingdom (v. 50).

There are marvelous implications to the truth of the resurrection. Those who have predeceased us in Christ are not gone forever. There will be a glorious reunion. This even makes a difference in the joys and pains of our current lives. As a father of five children, I am filled with joy knowing that I will have an eternity with my family. We will always have each other in the marvelous presence of our loving and caring eternal Father!

Having discussed the ideas of what a resurrection body will be like, Paul then moves to the subject of how the resurrection will happen. The change will not be gradual. It will happen in the blink of an eye (v. 51). The transformation will come at the end of days, and the perishable will become imperishable, the mortal become immortal (v. 53). This resurrection will be the final destruction of the power of death. Victory will swallow death (vv. 54-55).

Death is inevitable, but beyond it is the equally inevitable eternity; this is the true destiny for all who are found in Christ. Regarding this, Paul wrote to the Ephesians,

> I do not cease to give thanks for you, remembering you in my prayers, that the God of our Lord Jesus Christ, the Father of glory, may give you the Spirit of wisdom and of revelation in the knowledge of him, having the eyes of your hearts enlightened, that you may know what is the hope to which he has called you, what are the riches of his glorious inheritance in the saints, and what is the immeasurable greatness of his power toward us who believe, according to the working of his great might that he worked in Christ when he raised him from the dead and seated him at his right hand in the heavenly places, far above all rule and authority and power and dominion, and above every name that is named, not only in this age but also in the one to come. And he put all things under his feet and gave him as head over all things to the church, which is his body, the fullness of him who fills all in all. (Eph 1:16-23)

For Paul's readers to argue against a resurrection was, in Paul's mind, tantamount to arguing against God. God has reached out to take humanity into eternity. This was accomplished by the death and resurrection of Jesus Christ. May we all take refuge in God and his redemptive work, even as he transforms our lives until the day of our resurrection.

12

Closing Argument

IN THE FAMOUS CRIMINAL TRIAL of O. J. Simpson (1994–1995), defense attorney Johnny Cochran stood in front of the jury and handled a now famous glove. This was the glove that the prosecution contended was worn by the killer of Nicole Brown Simpson and Ron Goldman. The prosecution had challenged Simpson to put on the glove in front of the jury. The defense attorneys argued to the court that Simpson should not have to put his hand into a glove worn by a killer, but the court relented, letting Simpson first don a skintight latex glove before trying on the leather glove connected to the murder.

Simpson tried pulling the leather glove on his hand, but the glove did not fit. In his closing argument Cochran handled the glove and actually started pulling it onto his own hand. While doing so, Cochran uttered the phrase that is likely the most memorable line of the trial, "If the glove don't fit, you must acquit!"

Whether rightly or wrongly, the jury did so.

This trial brings me to the two major points I make in my closing argument. One centers on you as a juror. The other centers on the evidence.

As a trial lawyer of three decades and countless courtrooms, I can tell you with little doubt why the O. J. Simpson case was decided as it was. I believe that the jury would not convict Mr. Simpson as long as there was a conceivable argument that worked toward his innocence. I believe that the greater evidence dictated conviction, yet that jury disregarded that evidence in what the law calls "jury nullification," which means that the law or evidence is ignored because the jury has another agenda driving their verdict.

History will show that the Simpson trial came at a time of extreme racial hostility and unrest in Los Angeles, especially between the African American community and the Los Angeles police force. The police force was associated with the Rodney King beating (1991), racial profiling, falsifying evidence and more. The jury's verdict made a statement driven by things beyond the Simpson case.

This same concern arises for the religious issues set out in this book. It is difficult to set aside our preconceived ideas and emotions. For many, Christianity is associated with ugliness, hatred, harsh judgmentalism and closed-mindedness. For some, Christianity is out of touch with the expanding knowledge of the twenty-first century. Others associate Christianity with a moral code that represents a nice living standard. Still others see Christianity as one religion among many that all provide meaning in life and perhaps after death. Finally, there are those who follow the Christian faith blindly, whether it makes sense or not.

These attitudes need to be checked at the door for this closing argument. They all carry a bias that would stop someone from fairly considering the evidence offered in this book. It is the very kind of bias that causes the jury system to run amuck, bringing results that do not always reflect the truth.

My plea in this argument is to look at the evidence to see if there are some commonsense conclusions we can embrace. I ask for serious consideration of the ideas presented in this book, based not on preconceived notions but on common sense, which leads me to my second point from the Simpson trial.

Cochran's refrain, "If the glove don't fit, you must acquit," is sensible. In that case the argument is open to the counter that Simpson never tried on the glove itself. Simpson tried the glove over a latex glove. Arguably if the leather glove had fit over the other glove, one should acquit, because it would mean the leather glove was too large. But Cochran used a commonsense argument—one that we rightly consider. How does the evidence fit, in light of what we have experienced? Let's review the case.

We began by exploring the reasonableness of believing in God. God's existence makes sense in the world we live in. It explains why we sense right and wrong. It explains why we value human life. It explains why we are disturbed by injustice. Circumstantial evidence for the existence of God weighs heavily in favor of faith.

From there, we contemplated the biblical view of God, weighing it against reality. We saw that the Bible describes God as infinite, personal and moral. That God is infinite means he far exceeds what we can readily understand. The idea that God holds the vast universe in the palm of his hand (a figure of speech) explodes our ideas of God. There is no way we can understand such a God, except as he reveals himself to us.

The biblical God is also personal. God is not a supercomputer or a force; he desires a relationship with humans. God made woman and man to be in fellowship with him. And the redemptive act of Jesus is targeted at restoring relationships between people and God.

God is moral. That God embodies moral traits of truth, love and justice explains why these values reverberate not only in our own souls but throughout the universe. We innately cry out at injustice, value honesty, and desire to love and be loved. Our lives bear truth to the morality of a Creator God.

We also know from experience that we choose between alternatives. We make choices that are not always in line with the true moral good. Our immoral choices drive a wedge between the divine moral standard and us. We need help to overcome this wedge in order to have fellowship with God. This is where the work of Jesus comes into play. Jesus' incarnation, death and resurrection reveal that the loving, infinite God cares deeply about humans. They mean we are important. The One beyond comprehension deemed us worthy of his love. It means that he personally cares—enough to get involved at the cost of his own sacrifice and loss.

How do we know these things? We certainly did not figure them out on our own. God revealed them to us. He set forth these truths in a medium (words) we can understand. Through history, poetry, epistles and stories, the Bible sets out truths that make sense. They explain the values we hold, the struggles we face and the beauty we contemplate and hope for.

Understanding this story makes sense of the hope within us even though we face death. We are made for more than this life. We have a destiny, and that brings us back to my first point in the closing argument. We are not just a jury; we are the people in the case. The case is really about each of us. The real question behind this case is, What shall we do in regard to this God?

My answer? I accept this God. He has given reason for who I am and what I do. He has charged me with a sense of purpose. I long to hear from the personal and infinite God each day. I enjoy the blessings and privileges that flow from his answers to my responsive prayers. God's communication is not a monologue. He has initiated a dialogue in which I speak to him as I seek his will for my life. It changes the way I see my shortcomings and sins, not excusing them, but not letting them hinder my life by the weight of guilt. Instead, with praise for the forgiveness that was bought by the life and death of Christ, I venture forth in spite of my failures, seeking to forgive others their errors against me, just as I have experienced his forgiveness. I also live with my joy firmly planted in the confidence of eternity shared with him and others who have embraced the opportunities revealed and guaranteed by such a wonderful God.

That is the verdict I have reached. I think it is most reasonable, and I pray you do too.

NOTES

CHAPTER 2: GOD? GODS? OR NOTHING?

[1]Gilbert Keith Chesterton, *Tremendous Trifles* (Chester Springs, PA: Dufour, 1968), p. 55.

[2]Jean-Noel Biraben, "An Essay Concerning Mankind's Evolution," *Population: Selected Papers*, vol. 4 (Paris: National Institute for Population Studies, 1980).

[3]"Epic of Creation (Enuma Elish)," trans. Benjamin R. Foster, in *The Context of Scripture: Canonical Compositions from the Biblical World*, ed. William Hallo (London: Brill, 1996), 1:400.

[4]"Atra-Hasis," in Hallo, *Context of Scripture*, pp. 450-51.

[5]"The Wrath of Telipinu," trans. Gary Beckman, in Hallo, *Context of Scripture*, p. 151.

[6]C. S. Lewis, *The Weight of Glory and Other Addresses* (New York: Harper, 1949), p. 224.

CHAPTER 3: WHO GOD IS NOT!

[1]J. B. Phillips, *Your God Is Too Small* (New York: Touchstone, 2004).

[2]Ibid., p. 7.

[3]Roman Kriotor, quoted in Steve Silberman, "Life After Darth," *Wired*, May 2005, p. 141.

[4]George Lucas, quote in Silberman, "Life After Darth," p. 141.

[5]Phillips, *Your God Is Too Small*, p. 35.

[6]Ibid., p. 37.

[7]Ibid., p. 50.

[8]Bart Ehrman, *Forged: Writing in the Name of God—Why the Bible's Authors Are Not Who We Think They Are* (New York: Harper, 2011), p. 4.

CHAPTER 4: WHO IS GOD? (PART ONE)

[1]Alan Baddeley, *Your Memory: A User's Guide* (Buffalo, NY: Firefly, 2004).

[2]Eric Chiasson and Steve McMillan, *Astronomy Today*, 7th ed. (Boston: Addison-Wesley, 2011), p. 8.

[3]Albert Einstein, quoted in Antonina Vallentin, *Einstein: A Biography* (London: Weidenfeld & Nicolson, 1954), p. 24.

[4]John Polkinghorne, *Quarks, Chaos and Christianity* (New York: Crossroad, 2005), pp. 35-36.

CHAPTER 5: WHO IS GOD? (PART TWO)

[1]John Polkinghorne, *Quarks, Chaos and Christianity* (New York: Crossroad, 2005), p. 10.

[2]Naveena Kottoor, "IBM Supercomputer Overtakes Fujitsu as World's Fastest," *BBC News*, June 18, 2012, www.bbc.co.uk/news/technology-18457716.

[3]Frank Close, *Particle Physics: A Very Short Introduction* (Oxford: Oxford University Press, 2004), pp. 1-6.

[4]Diogenes Laertius, *Lives of the Philosophers* 9.

[5]Heraclitus, *On the Universe* 57, trans. W. H. S. Jones, Loeb Classical Library (London: William Heineman, 1931).

[6]Ibid., 52.

[7]Ibid., 67.

[8]Ibid., 1-2.

[9]Aristotle, *Metaphysics* 987.a.32.

[10]Pseudo-Plato, *Hippias Major*, in *The Art and Thought of Heraclitus*, trans. Charles H. Kahn (Cambridge: Cambridge University Press, 1981), p. 55.

CHAPTER 6: BIOLINGUISTICS AND THE COMMUNICATING GOD

[1]Peter MacNeilage, *The Origin of Speech* (New York: Oxford University Press, 2010), p. 4.

[2]T. H. Huxley, *Man's Place in Nature* (1863). An interesting review of this book and its quote is found in the *Anthropological Review*, May 1863, beginning at page 107.

[3]This comment came in a lecture given in 1976 at an American Association for the Advancement of Science meeting. The lecture text can be found at the National Library of Medicine's "Profiles in Science" website: http://profiles.nlm.nih.gov/ps/access/QLBBHR.ocr.

[4]Cicero, *De Divinatione* 2.55.115.

[5]Ibid.

[6]*Didache*, chap. 8. Different scholars date the *Didache* as early as A.D. 50 to 125.

[7]See note 3 of this chapter.

CHAPTER 7: REALITY AND THE GOD OF TRUTH

[1]Plato, *The Republic*, bk. 7.

[2]Burton Watson, *The Complete Works of Chuang Tzu* (New York: Columbia University Press, 1968), chap. 2.

[3]Nick Bostrom, "Are You Living in a Computer Simulation?" *Philosophical Quarterly* 53, no. 211 (2003): 243-55.

[4]Richard Thaler and Cass Sunstein, *Nudge: Improving Decisions About Health, Wealth, and Happiness* (New York: Penguin, 2009).

[5]Augustine, *Tractates on the Gospel of John* 29.6.

CHAPTER 8: RIGHT, WRONG AND THE MORAL GOD

[1]William Shirer details this and much more history regarding Nazi Germany. See his *The Rise and Fall of the Third Reich* (New York: Fawcett, 1981), p. 233.

[2]"Nazi Conspiracy and Aggression" (Nuremberg Documents), V, pp. 341ff (N.D. 2620-PS).

[3]Ibid., V, pp. 696-99 (N.D. 2992-PS).

[4]Matthew White, *Atrocities: The 100 Deadliest Episodes in Human History* (New York: W. W. Norton, 2011), pp. 393-94, 495.

[5]See the State Department executive summary at "Ethnic Cleansing in Kosovo: An Accounting," U.S. State Department, December 1999, www .state.gov/www/global/human_rights/kosovoii/homepage.html.

[6]Friedrich Nietzsche, *Beyond Good and Evil*, trans. Marion Faber (Oxford: Oxford University Press, 2008), p. 8.

[7]Friedrich Nietzsche, *Thus Spoke Zarathustra*, trans. Graham Parkes (Oxford: Oxford University Press, 2005), pp. 250-51.

[8]In fairness to Darwin and Nietzsche, we should note that neither would likely have approved of Hitler's choices. Darwin's theory depended on species diversification, and genocide would not have fit well into his approach. Nietzsche was not anti-Semitic, and most scholars agree that the

anti-Semitic insertions in his writings were the work of his sister, who, along with her husband, were profoundly anti-Semitic.

[9]Friedrich Nietzsche, *Beyond Good and Evil: Prelude to a Philosphy of the Future*, trans. Helen Zimmern (New York: Macmillan, 1907), pp. 9-10.

[10]C. S. Lewis, *Christian Reflections* (Grand Rapids: Eerdmans, 1994), p. 79.

[11]Plato's story of this dialogue puts an ironic twist on the actions of the overly pious. Euthyphro is a "religious professional" who is taking his father to court in a manner that Greeks would have considered impious. Euthyphro tries to justify his actions by claiming they mimic the gods' actions in the traditional stories. Even the name Euthyphro (eu = "good," thy = "God," and phro = "to judge") mocks his actions. Euthyphro is one who is judging what is good to the gods, yet he clearly does not have a clue, at least as Plato relates the story.

[12]Norman Snaith, *The Distinctive Ideas of the Old Testament* (Peterborough, UK: Epworth, 1983), p. 59.

[13]Avi Sagi and Daniel Statman, *Religion and Morality* (Atlanta: Rodopi, 1995), p. 62.

[14]Katherine Rogers, *Anselm on Freedom* (Oxford: Oxford University Press, 2008), p. 8.

CHAPTER 9: FREE WILL, MORAL RESPONSIBILITY AND THE INFINITE, JUST GOD

[1]B. F. Skinner, *Beyond Freedom and Dignity* (New York: Knopf, 1971), p. 11.

[2]Ibid., p. 13.

[3]Ibid., p. 19.

[4]Ibid., p. 58.

[5]Ibid., p. 104.

[6]Steven J. Haggbloom et al., "The 100 Most Eminent Psychologists of the 20th Century," *Review of General Psychology* 6, no. 2 (June 2002): 139-52.

[7]Noam Chomsky, "The Case Against B. F. Skinner," *New York Review of Books*, December 30, 1971, www.chomsky.info/articles/19711230.htm.

[8]Ibid.

[9]Ibid.

CHAPTER 10: THE AUDACITY OF THE RESURRECTION

[1]These observations of jury behavior come from both the rules and laws

that govern jury trials as well as from the experience and practice of the author, a well-experienced trial lawyer.

[2] *The Martyrdom of Polycarp*, in *The Apostolic Fathers*, trans. J. B. Lightfoot and J. R. Harmer, ed. Michael W. Holmes, 2nd ed. (Grand Rapids: Baker, 1989).

[3] Josephus, *Antiquities of the Jews* 18.3.3, in Paul L. Maier, *Josephus: The Essential Works* (Grand Rapids: Kregel, 1994), p. 269. For over a century, scholars discussed whether Christians have added to parts of Josephus, making the passage more amenable to the Christian faith. In 1971 Hebrew University's noted Jewish scholar Shlomo Pines published on a discovered tenth-century Arabic copy of Josephus that seems to be thoroughly Jewish in its presentation. I have used this modified account rather than the full Christian account more typically used. For more details see ibid., p. 282 n. 8, and more fully, Shlomo Pines, *An Arabic Version of the Testimonium Flavianum and Its Implications* (Jerusalem: Jerusalem Academic Press, 1971).

[4] Tacitus, *Annals* 15.44, trans. John E. Jackson, Loeb Classical Library 322 (Cambridge, MA: Harvard University Press, 1937), p. 283.

[5] Pliny the Younger, *Epistles* 10.96.

[6] Seutonius misspelled Christ as "Chrest" (Lat. Chresto), writing, "Iudaeos impulsore Chresto assidue tumultuantis Roma expulit." The passage can be translated as, "He expelled the Jews because they created constant disturbances arising over Christ." Most scholars readily recognize that "Chrest" is indeed Christ because of its peculiarity as a Jewish name. Chrestus is not a typical Jewish name. For that matter, it is not a common Greek or Latin name either. It is a Latinized derivation of the Greek word for "anointed" (*Christos*), not the Hebrew word, which would be *Mashiach*. Instead, it seems to be an alternate spelling of Christus (Christ). This makes more sense remembering that the uniformity of modern spelling derives from the birth of dictionaries as well as the ready availability of printed materials, both products since the Renaissance. In ancient times spelling was based on pronunciation, and Chrest was a normal mispronunciation of Christ, as we see from the African lawyer Quintus Septimus Florens Tertullian (c. 160–c. 225), who wrote in defense of the Christian faith less than one hundred years later: "'Christian,' [Christianus] so far as translating goes, is derived from 'anointing.' Yes, and when it is mispronounced by you 'Chrestian' [Chres-

tianus] (for you have not even certain knowledge of the mere name)."
See Tertullian, *Apology* 3.5, trans T. R. Glover, Loeb Classical Library 250
(Cambridge, MA: Harvard University Press, 1997).

[7]Clement of Alexandria, quoted in Eusebius, *Ecclesiastical History* 2.9.2.

[8]Hegesippus, quoted in Eusebius, *Ecclesiastical History* 2.23.

[9]There are ancient accounts that assert that Mark was an eyewitness, and
scholars point to subtle clues in his Gospel that can be read to support
such an idea. But Mark's Gospel makes no clear claim to being an eyewitness account. Hence a court would treat it as hearsay, and so do I. That
does not mean it isn't reliable or true. It simply means it is not admissible
in a court of evidence.

[10]Charles Colson, *Breakpoint Online Commentary*, April 29, 2002, www
.breakpoint.org/commentaries/4187-an-unholy-hoax.

CHAPTER 11: DEATH AND ETERNITY

[1]David Ropeik and George Gray, *Risk: A Practical Guide for Deciding What's
Really Safe and What's Really Dangerous in the World Around You* (New
York: Houghton Mifflin, 2002), pp. 421-25.

[2]Gordon Fee, *The First Epistle to the Corinthians*, New International Commentary on the New Testament (Grand Rapids: Eerdmans, 1987), p. 741.

[3]Ibid., p. 760.